NUMBER
The Making of
Constitution Hill
FOUR

NUMBER
The Making of
Constitution Hill
FOUR

PENGUIN GROUP

PENGUIN BOOKS

Published by the Penguin Group
Penguin Books Ltd, 80 Strand, London WC2R 0RL, England
Penguin Group (USA) Inc, 375 Hudson Street, New York, New York 10014, USA
Penguin Group (Canada), 90 Eglinton Avenue East, Suite 700, Toronto, Ontario, M4P 2Y3, Canada (a division of Pearson Penguin Canada Inc.)
Penguin Ireland, 25 St Stephen's Green, Dublin 2, Ireland (a division of Penguin Books Ltd)
Penguin Group (Australia), 250 Camberwell Road, Camberwell, Victoria 3124, Australia (a division of Pearson Australia Group Pty Ltd)
Penguin Books India Pvt Ltd, 11 Community Centre, Panchsheel Park, New Delhi – 110 017, India
Penguin Group (NZ), Cnr Rosedale and Airborne Roads, Albany, Auckland 1310, New Zealand (a division of Pearson New Zealand Ltd)
Penguin Books (South Africa) (Pty) Ltd, 24 Sturdee Avenue, Rosebank, Johannesburg 2196, South Africa

Penguin Books (South Africa) (Pty) Ltd, Registered Offices:
24 Sturdee Avenue, Rosebank, Johannesburg 2196, South Africa

www.penguinbooks.co.za

First published in 2006

ISBN 0 143 02498 1

Design and typesetting by: **Bon–Bon**
Cover photograph: **Adam Broomberg and Oliver Chanarin**
Chapter divider photographs: **John Hodgkiss and Guto Bussab**
Cover design: **Carina Comrie**
Printed and bound by: **CTP Book Printers, Cape Town**

Contents

Acknowledgements

This book has been a collective effort that has drawn on the expertise and talents of a great number of people. The project has been steered by an editorial team who have read countless drafts and made invaluable suggestions. Editorial team members are Graeme Reid, Brian Orlin, Tshepo Nkosi, Mark Gevisser, Steve Kwena Mokwena, Herbert Prins and Mike Freedman. Judge Albie Sachs has tirelessly given of his time, his eloquence and his enthusiasm and has shaped many aspects of the book. Other Judges of the Constitutional Court - Justice Kate O'Regan, Justice Johann Kriegler and Justice Yvonne Mokgoro – have been extremely helpful throughout the process. Janina Masojada and Paul Wygers have been very generous in helping with the sections on Constitutional Court. Neil Fraser has helped considerably on the sections on the inner city. Gavin Stafford, Stan Joseph and Samantha Naidoo at Ochre Media have provided a secure home for the project. Carina Camrie has been a dream designer to work with.

The team at Penguin has provided an incredible opportunity for the story of Constitution Hill to be told. They have supported the project each step of the way and offered their considerable expertise.

This book would not have been possible without the generous support of Atlantic Philanthropies and in particular, Gerald Kraak, who has believed in Constitution Hill from the start.

The book relies on interviews with the many people who have been involved in the making of Constitution Hill. Particular thanks goes to the ex-prisoners of Number Four who have taken the courage to remember and to share their experiences of the jail with visitors to the Hill and the readers of this book. This book is dedicated to their resilience, and to the triumph of the human spirit.

Contributors
Project Manager: Lauren Segal
Writers and Editors: Lauren Segal (lead writer), Karen Martin, Sharon Cort
Photographic Curator: Sharon Cort
Designers: Carina Comrie and Adele Prins from Bon-Bon
Design Supervisor: Clive van den Berg
Archivists: Churchill Madikida, Nomsa Khumalo, Cheryl Stevens
Researchers: Cheryl Stevens (lead researcher), Nikiwe Deborah Matshoba
Editors: Jane Ranger (lead editor), Pam Thornley and Sandy Shoolman
Transcriber: Joan Appel

Lauren Segal

Foreword

When the interim Constitution was adopted in 1994, a new order had been ushered in and South Africa would never be the same again. The prolonged period of oppression and authoritarianism had passed. Its place had been taken by a new constitutional order founded on values including human dignity, the achievement of equality, the advancement of human rights and freedoms, non-racialism and non-sexism and the rule law.

The ideals espoused by both the interim and the final Constitutions have been expressed explicitly enough. They recall the struggles of the people of South Africa to rid themselves of a past of deep divisions 'characterised by strife, conflict, untold suffering and injustice' in order to achieve the ideal of 'a society based on democratic values, social justice and fundamental human rights ... an open society in which government is based on the will of the people and every citizen is equally protected by law...'

Nowhere are these struggles of the past and the ideals espoused in our basic law better and more poignantly expressed than in the siting of the Constitutional Court and the development of Constitution Hill. Paging through the pages of this book is a journey through division, prejudice and suffering; it is a depiction of heroism and a refusal to submit to oppression; it is finally an eloquent and graphic expression of the triumph of the South African people over adversity. These pages are a celebration of how the worst that South Africa had been has been turned into a great symbol of freedom and hope, presaging the best that humanity can offer.

CHIEF JUSTICE PIUS LANGA
DECEMBER 2005

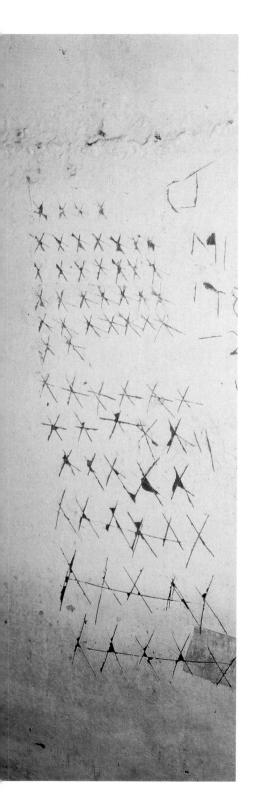

Introduction

The Old Fort Prison complex – commonly known as Number Four – is one of the oldest remaining buildings in the rapidly changing landscape of Johannesburg. Virtually every important political leader in South African history from Mahatma Gandhi to Nelson Mandela as well as scores of ordinary South Africans caught in the web of colonial and apartheid repression, have been imprisoned in these jails. The old stonewalls tell a century's worth of stories of an iniquitous political system, a brutal penal institution, and the resilience of generations of prisoners.

When the jails closed in 1983, the site lay abandoned for many years. In 1996, the judges of the new Constitutional Court announced that this notorious prison complex was to become the home of the Constitutional Court – a bold decision, highly symbolic of the extent to which the hopes for the new South Africa are built on, and honour, the pain of the past.

Since that momentous announcement, Number Four has undergone a remarkable process of transformation. It has become Constitution Hill, a major inner-city regeneration project and a thriving mixed-use precinct with the Constitutional Court as an anchor surrounded by the old prison buildings. Constitution Hill embodies the drama of the changes that have taken place in our country as well as the dreams, hopes and imaginings for the future.

This book tells the story of the making of Constitution Hill from the time that the prison was abandoned until the present. The book stops at some of the important junctures along the way:

the abandonment and the decay of the old colonial and apartheid buildings during a strange period of hiatus

the rescue of the site by the visionary Constitutional Court judges who sought a home for their new court

the design of an innovative Court that created a new ethos for South African buildings and public spaces

the leap of faith taken by the Johannesburg City Council and developers who saw the potential of the site for inner city regeneration

the arrival of heritage makers who teased the ghosts out of the crevices of the stonework

the return of the prisoners who courageously came back to tell their stories

the reclamation of the space by the public

There was no substantial or organised record of these moments in history. The book has been a process of trawling, excavating, scavenging, listening, recording, learning and discovering. The archival fragments that have emerged, and the interviews that have been conducted have suggested new ways of seeing and understanding the story of the site. The material has been stitched together into a loose narrative that reflects the energy and diversity of the people who have shaped and developed this site. Many dreamed Constitution Hill into existence. From warders to ex-prisoners to judges, from government officials to builders, from architects, artisans and artists to heritage lovers, all are part of the story.

Like Constitution Hill, this book is layered and textured. The ellipses in the text, like the ghosts that occupy the prison, often speak as powerfully as the words on the page. The book officially ends with the opening of the Women's Jail in 2005 but the journey of the making of the Hill continues. As the site continues to grow as a public space, new layers of meaning and interpretation will be added. This remarkable place will undoubtedly continue to develop and change throughout the course of the 21st century.

A vision for Constitution Hill

Constitution Hill is a very specific geological place

it is a watershed
it is a fault line that contained immense wealth
it is a vantage point

Constitution Hill is a very specific geographical place

it is in Africa
it is in South Africa
it is in the heart of the City of Johannesburg
the City of Johannesburg is at the heart of South Africa

The Hill, its Fort and its Gaol contain the twentieth century in South Africa

It is a political place
a fortified place
a colonial place
a garrison place
an African place
a Boer place
a British place
an apartheid place

It is a place of inspiration
a place of solidarity
a place of thinking
a place of discovery
a place of stories
a place of singing
a place of greatness

It is a terrible place
a place of injustice and brutality
a place of separation and segregation
a place of sickness and suffering
a place of isolation and overcrowding
a place of fear and torture
a place of rape and murder

As it stands today Constitution Hill is

an unknown place, an invisible place, an unacknowledged place – to most

a visited place, a place to fear, an intimately known place – to others

yet another piece of another generation's history – to many of the young

an overlooked place

an overlooking place

a building site in waiting

an internationally important heritage site

a place with immense potential to inform, stimulate, educate, move and change visitors from Johannesburg, the country and the rest of the world

a place with a significant economic contribution to make

a place for the people of Johannesburg and South Africa to be proud of

From 'Notes towards a Concept Outline', Peter Stark, Centre for Cultural Policy and Management, University of Northumbria, April 2001

When completed Constitution Hill will be

an internationally important symbol of
the new South Africa

born of the political process but now independent of it

the home of the Law of the Constitution

the home of the guarantor of Human Rights
for every South African citizen

a working place
an ordinary place
an urban place
a complex place

a place of stories
a place of history
a place of triumph
a barren place

an extraordinary place
a place of contradictions
a place of resolution
a place of justice

a place of reflection
a place of sorrow
a place of hope
a place of simplicity

a place of study
a place of learning
a place of art
a place of flowers

an everyday place
at the heart of Johannesburg
at the heart of the constitution
at the heart of a new South Africa

BOYS
STAND ...
DELIVER
DIE
OR

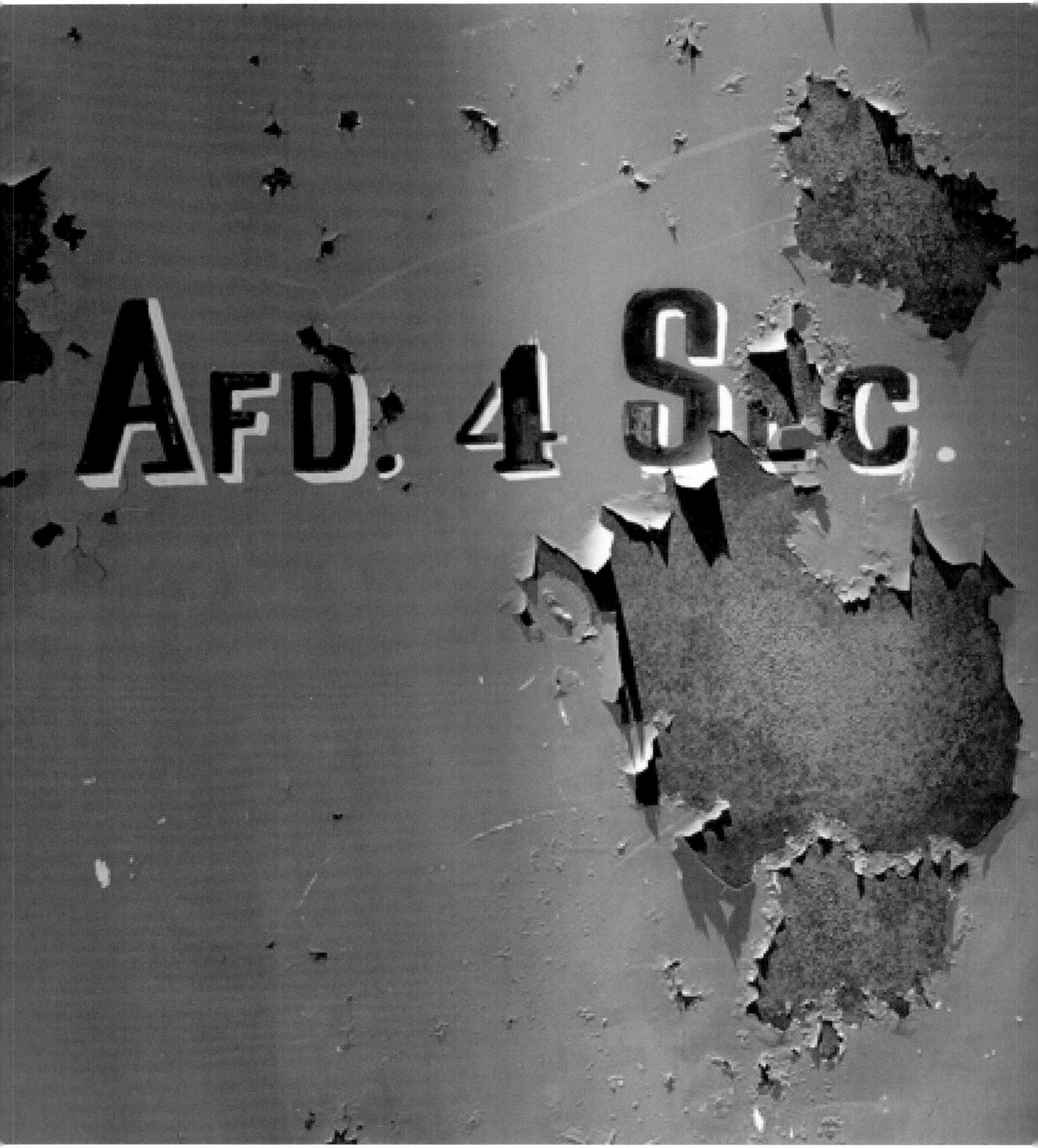
AFD. 4

List of Abbreviations

ANC	African National Congress
ATB	Awaiting Trial Block
CCB	Civil Co-operation Bureau
CEO	Chief Executive Officer
CJP	Central Johannesburg Partnership
CODESA	Convention for a Democratic South Africa
CGE	Commission on Gender Equality
CRL	Commission for the Promotion and Protection of Rights of Cultural, Religious and Linguistic Communities
DACST	Department of Arts Culture Science and Technology
DPW	Department of Public Works
HET	Heritage, Education and Tourism
HRC	Human Rights Commission
IEC	Independent Electoral Commission
JDA	Johannesburg Development Agency
JMC	Johannesburg Metropolitan Council
NMC	National Monuments Council
OPP	Office of the Public Protector
PAC	Pan African Congress
RLI	Rand Light Infantry
SAHRC	South African Human Rights Commission
SAHRA	South African Heritage Resources Agency
SAIA	South African Institute of Architects
WTP	We The People
WSSD	World Summit for Sustainable Development

Perceptions of Number Four

White people were largely ignorant of what took place behind the high rampart walls of the Fort. For the black population of Joburg, however, the prisons were notorious. Referred to simply as Number Four, the different prisons on the site evoked terror amongst generations of black people. At least one member of almost every family living in the townships around the city disappeared into Number Four for a period of time and many heartbreaking stories are told of the horrors that took place there. Number Four came to symbolise the cruelties and indignities of colonialism and apartheid as well as the courage and resilience of the black community. Number Four lives on in the popular imagination - taxis are still told to stop at Number Four when coming to this part of town.

For the Europeans, conditions were as they are in British remand prisons. But the non-Europeans know the Fort as the Little Hell.

Lionel Forman and Solly Sachs, SAHRA report

My grandmother had taught us to say goodbye when we went to shop in town, because we never knew if we would come back or not. We used to say, 'If you don't see me, check for me at Number Four.'

Nolundi Ntamo, pass offender

We knew Number Four to be a very scary place, like going down a mine. When the police car arrived at the reception, you used to go deep, deep, deep into the earth.

Sipho Sibiya, ex-political prisoner

They told you that your life was over beyond the gate of the prison.

Nolundi Ntamo, pass offender

They made prisoners of the most respectable people, for nothing.

Jeannie Noel, ex-political prisoner

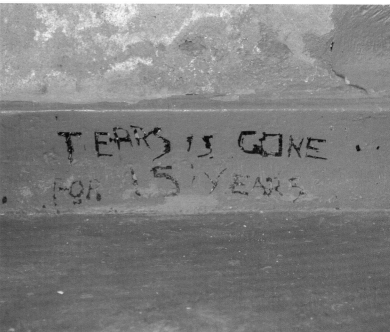

Most of us look upon the Fort merely as the place to telephone as a last resort when our local police stations cannot tell us the whereabouts of our servants arrested on petty pass laws or so-called trespass offences.

Letter to The Star, 9 December 1964

I grew up terrified of Number Four. I heard many stories of anguish from people who had been locked up in this god-forsaken place. It was an urban rite of passage for thousands of young black men and women growing up in a sick society.

Steve Kwena Mokwena, curator

ISOLATION CELLS, DOORS OF ISOLATION CELLS, WOMEN'S JAIL ATRIUM Andrew Meintjes **GRAFFITI IN NUMBER FOUR** John Hodgkiss

Orientation Map
2004

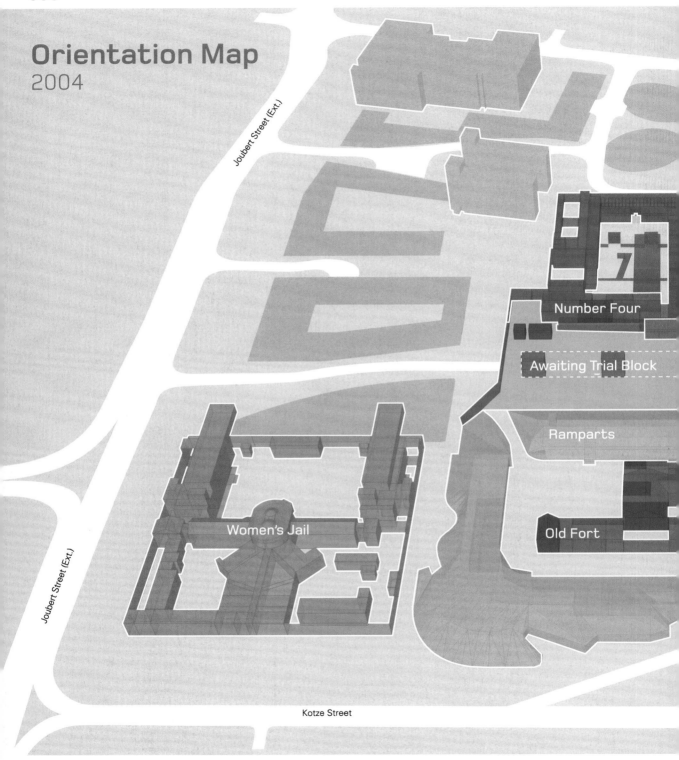

Joubert Street (Ext.)

Number Four

Awaiting Trial Block

Ramparts

Women's Jail

Old Fort

Joubert Street (Ext.)

Kotze Street

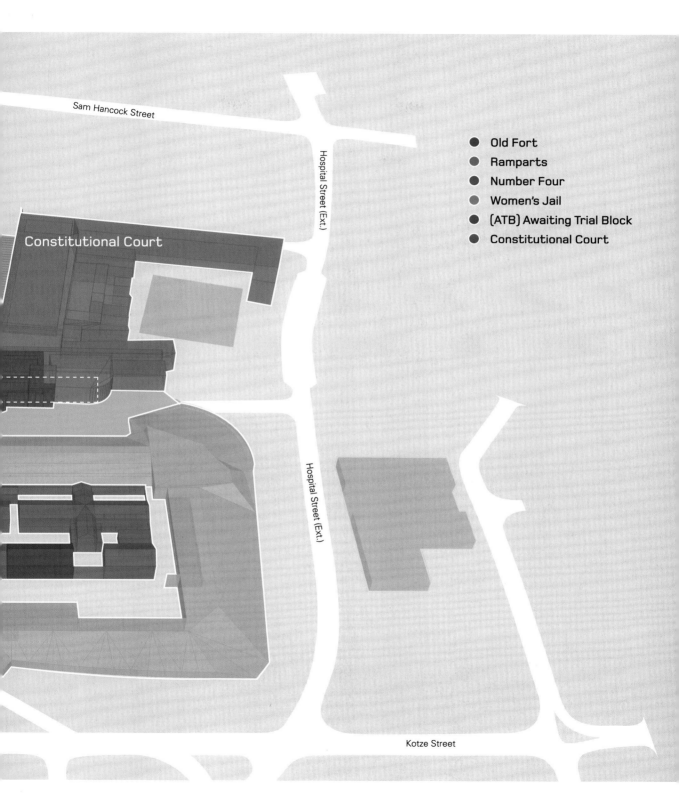

Sam Hancock Street

Hospital Street (Ext.)

Constitutional Court

Hospital Street (Ext.)

Kotze Street

● Old Fort
● Ramparts
● Number Four
● Women's Jail
● (ATB) Awaiting Trial Block
● Constitutional Court

Chronology

1893

Paul Kruger, the president of the Zuid-Afrikaansche Republiek (ZAR), built the first high-security prison on a strategic hill overlooking Johannesburg to keep control over the *uitlanders* (foreigners) in the mining village below.

1896

Kruger turned the newly built prison into a military fort after the Jameson Raid of 1896, when mainly English-speaking immigrants attempted to overthrow the Boer government.

1899

After the outbreak of the South African War (Anglo-Boer War), the Boers kept watch over developments from the rampart walls. Artillery was stored in rooms beneath the ramparts.

1900

The British took occupation of Johannesburg. The Boers handed the British the keys of the Old Fort.

1902

After the war ended, the Public Works Department authorised the Fort's temporary use as a prison pending the erection of a new jail. The Johannesburg City Council was opposed to a prison in the middle of a growing residential area. But this temporary arrangement was to stay in place for the next 80 years.

1904

The 'native' prison, better known as Number Four, was built outside of the rampart walls to accommodate convicted black male prisoners.

1910

A new Women's Jail was built. The Victorian building held white and black women in separate sections.

1928

The Awaiting Trial Block was built to house male, black awaiting trial prisoners.

1948

The Nationalist government was voted into power and an increasing number of people were incarcerated as a result of apartheid laws. The prisons were severely overcrowded.

1964

Amidst much controversy as to whether a prison site was worthy of such a title, the Old Fort was proclaimed a National Monument.

1983

On 31 January 1983, nearly one hundred years after the Old Fort was built, all prisoners were transferred to the new Diepkloof prison (Sun City) outside Soweto.

1990

Funding to turn the Old Fort into a prison museum did not materialise. Parts of the Old Fort and Women's Jail continued to be occupied but as a whole, the site was neglected and all but forgotten.

1994

The Constitutional Court was established as a completely new court by the interim constitution of 1993. President Mandela inaugurated the Constitutional Court on 14 February 1995.

1996

Having occupied temporary accommodation since 1994, the judges looked at a number of sites for the new court building. They chose the site of the prisons partly because of its accessibility and sense of space but primarily because of its historical and symbolical importance.

1998

The anonymous competition to design the court building was won by OMM Design Workshop in partnership with Urban Solutions.

2001

New impetus was given to the project when Blue IQ, established by the Provincial Government to turn Gauteng into a smart province, assisted with the financing for the court. The JDA, a city-wide economic development agency, became responsible for the completion of the court building and the development of Constitution Hill as a major heritage site.

2004

The court moved into its new home in February. President Thabo Mbeki inaugurated the court on Human Rights Day, 21 March 2004. Constitution Hill opened to the public from 22 March 2004.

2006

All planned elements of the mixed-use development at Constitution Hill are estimated to be complete by the end of 2007.

Political Prisoners

1900

Boers and pro-Boer sympathisers, like James Thompson Bain, were imprisoned after the British took control of Johannesburg. Cornelis Broeksma, David Garnius Wernick and Burger Vermaak were executed in the courtyard of the Old Fort.

1908

Mahatma Gandhi, leader of the Passive Resistance Movement against the Pass Laws for Asians (Satyagraha), was jailed with many other Indians for refusing to carry a pass.

1913

White mineworkers were jailed for going on strike.

1922

A group of white miners were imprisoned after they had armed themselves and seized most of Johannesburg during the 1922 miners' strike.

1942

Members of the Ossewa Brandwag, a staunch Afrikaner nationalist and pro-Nazi group, were jailed for acts of violence and sabotage during World War Two.

1914

General Christiaan de Wet and his followers were jailed for leading the rebellion against the entry of the Union of South Africa into World War One on the side of Great Britain.

1955

Participants in the Defiance Campaign, led by the ANC to fight against apartheid laws, were jailed after signing the Freedom Charter.

1956

Many of the 156 treason trialists, including Nelson Mandela, Albert Luthuli, Joe Slovo, ZK Mathews, Walter Sisulu, Oliver Tambo, Helen Joseph, Moses Kotane, Lilian Ngoyi and Ruth First, were imprisoned in the Old Fort, the Awaiting Trial Block and the Women's Jail.

1958

Albertina Sisulu and Winnie Madikizela-Mandela were among the hundreds of women imprisoned for protesting against the pass laws.

1960

Robert Sobukwe, leader of the Pan African Congress (PAC), as well as other anti-pass campaigners were arrested and imprisoned after marching to the Orlando Police Station.

1960

Scores of activists were imprisoned under the State of Emergency, including Joe Slovo, Reverend Douglas Thompson, Rica Hodgson, Violet Weinberg and Rusty Bernstein.

1976

Tens of students were detained during the Soweto Uprising as well as leaders of organisations including Fatima Meer, Winnie Madikizela-Mandela, Nomakhaya 'Kayo' Ethel Mafuna, Oshadi Mangena-Phakathi, Nikiwe Deborah Matshoba, Mapitso Lolo Tabane, Cecilie Palmer, Vesta Smith, Joyce Piliso Seroke, Jeannie Noel, Sally Motlana, Sibongile Kubeka.

1964

A group of 'suspected communists', including Esther and Hymie Barsel, Ivan Schermbrucker, Eli Weinberg, Norman Levy, Constantinos Gazides, Paul Henry Trewhela, Lewis Baker, Jean Strachan, Anne Nicholson, Sylvia Neam, Florence Duncan, Mollie Irene Doyle, were imprisoned.

1980

Activists accused of treason in the early 1980s who were imprisoned included Alan Fine, Rob Adams, Barbara Hogan, Hanchen Koornhof, Lillian Keagile, Joe Thloloe and Reverend Cedric Mayson.

POSTCARD OF THE FORT, EARLY 1900s MuseuMAfricA

The Prison Buildings

a historical overview
1883–1983

e of the Fort.

The Old Fort

Johannesburg had only been established for seven years when Paul Kruger, president of the Zuid-Afrikaansche Republiek, built the Fort in 1893. This high-security jail, situated on a high ridge north of the town, was intended to intimidate and keep control of the *uitlanders* (foreigners) in the mining town of Johannesburg. Kruger turned the newly built prison into a military fort after the Jameson Raid of 1896, when mainly English-speaking immigrants conspired with the British to overthrow the Boer government. With the advent of the South African War (Anglo-Boer War) in 1899, the Boer *Staatsartillerie* kept a sharp eye on developments from their perch high on Hospital Hill. But when the British took occupation of Johannesburg in May 1900, the Fort was surrendered without a shot and the British army imprisoned Boer soldiers in their own Fort. This marked the beginning of the long history of the Fort as a place of punishment, confinement and abuse of prisoners of all political persuasions.

Once the war was over, in 1902, the Fort reverted to a prison again, and was Johannesburg's main place of incarceration of prisoners for eight decades. The jail always had a brooding presence in the city, especially as the elegant suburb of Hospital Hill grew around it. Over the years it became known as the Old Fort.

THE JOHANNESBURG JAIL BEFORE THE RAMPARTS WERE BUILT, MID – 1890s Cape Town Archives Repository

SOLDIERS ON PARADE AFTER THE RAMPARTS WERE BUILT, EARLY 1900s Cape Town Archives Repository

Hillbrow & the Fort from Parktown
looking up Banket Street, Johannesburg.

The Fort.

VIEW OF THE FORT IN EARLY JOHANNESBURG LANDSCAPE MuseuMAfricA

The superb ridge, which seemed to me with its beautiful houses and gardens a veritable Paradise and which would certainly be an ornament to any city on the globe, had in its centre a large and ugly earthwork, behind which were monstrous Krupp guns to lay waste this Eden, should the humanity of Johannesburg ever be driven by despair to strive physically for the right of freemen. The mere suggestion of it is brutish, and a Government which can coolly contemplate such a possibility, and frighten timid women and young children with such horrid prospects, is only fit to be classed with the Herods of the Dark Ages.

Henry Stanley, explorer and journalist, circa 1897

The Ramparts

In 1896, the ramparts were built around the prison to bolster the military defences of the Kruger government after the Jameson Raid. The ramparts contained two bastions, one overlooking the town of Johannesburg to the south and one to the north guarding the road to Pretoria. Gunfire could be directed at anyone attempting to seize the city by force. The rooms within the rampart walls were used to store the guns and ammunition, first of the Boer soldiers and then of the British. The British made extensive use of the ramparts as a viewpoint after their occupation of the Fort in 1900.

When the South African War ended in 1902 and the Old Fort became a prison again, the underground rooms were used as offices, recreation rooms and quarters for unmarried warders. Between 1902 and 1983, the ramparts functioned as prison walls. They hid what was happening inside the Old Fort and blocked both common criminals and political prisoners off from the rest of society.

No longer needed for surveillance, intimidation or incarceration, the ramparts now serve as a vantage point over Constitution Hill, the city of Johannesburg, and South Africa in the process of transition. They serve as a bridge between the difficulties of the past – as represented by the derelict old prison buildings – and the possibilities of the future – as represented by the Constitutional Court.

MEN ON THE RAMPARTS National Archives and Records Service of South Africa

Number Four

From the beginning of the Fort's history as a prison, white inmates were kept within the rampart walls, while black inmates were held outside. In 1902, Sections Four and Five were built to house sentenced black male prisoners.

Number Four's large communal cells held violent criminals, pass offenders and political prisoners side by side. The cells were hugely overcrowded and the treatment of prisoners was extremely brutal. The *ekhulukhuthu* or isolation cells were used to punish those who had committed an offence inside the prison. The steel doors of the punishment cells are covered in graffiti, and contain an evocative record of the lives, fears and aspirations of the thousands of men who were held here over the decades.

The mats are filthy, the blankets are filthy, the latrines are filthy, the food is filthy, the utensils are filthy, the convicts' clothes are filthy. The latrines overflowed and made a stench.

Alex La Guma, ex-political prisoner, 1956

IMAGE OF NUMBER FOUR TAKEN FROM ADJACENT BUILDING Bob Gosani, Bailey's African History Archive

'Strip!'
We took off our clothes and
stood stark naked in
the yard of the Fort ... a
dreadful, crumbling place
of incarceration for thousands
of prisoners awaiting trial or
newly convicted. The warders
mocked us for the nakedness
they had ordered.

'*Tausa*'
We refused, we had seen other
prisoners doing the *tausa* and
we were not going to do it. A
naked person leapt in the air,
spinning round and opening
his legs wide while clapping
his hands overhead and then,
in the same moment, coming
down, making clicking sounds
with the mouth and bending
his body right forward so as to
expose an open rectum to the
warder's inspection.

Indres Naidoo, *Island in Chains*

A PRISONER IN NUMBER FOUR UNDERGOING THE TAUSA, A HUMILIATING BODY SEARCH Bob Gosani, Bailey's African History Archive

The Women's Jail

The Women's Jail was built in 1910. For seventy-three years, it imprisoned thousands of women who came to Johannesburg to try and make a living. Some were arrested for crimes such as shoplifting, prostitution, fraud and murder. Many others were detained for protesting against the system of apartheid. But the vast majority were ordinary black women, arrested for not carrying a pass, for trespassing or for contravening one of the many apartheid laws. These black women were regarded as criminals because of the colour of their skin. White and black women were held in separate sections of the jail.

Most inmates were short-term prisoners with sentences of less than three months. At times, they had small children or babies with them and the prison was extremely overcrowded.

WOMEN'S JAIL ATRIUM Andrew Meintjes

A stairway bearing evidence of past grandeur swept by a circular gallery with a wrought iron railing to the first floor. I had a fleeting vision of Victorian ladies looking down on the ball in progress, but was jolted into the reality of the prison by a line of stark naked women, their arms outstretched, being searched, by a *vagaash* (black warder).

Fatima Meer, ex-political prisoner, Prison Diary: 113 Days

WOMEN'S JAIL ENTRANCE Loren Barale

A DOMESTIC WORKER BEING ARRESTED FOR A PASS OFFENCE Eli Weinberg, UWC Robben Island Museum, Mayibuye Archives

I can't believe that they arrested me simply because I did not have my pass on me. There I was with meat and mealie meal in a bag being searched and sworn at and taken to prison.

Sarah Sematlane, pass offender

ONE OF THE ONLY IMAGES OF THE AWAITING TRIAL BLOCK TAKEN IN 1954 WHILST IT WAS STILL IN OPERATION AS A PRISON Bailey's African History Archive

The Awaiting Trial Block

The Awaiting Trial Block (ATB) was built in 1928. Tens of thousands of men passed through its large and overcrowded communal cells.

Political prisoners – the treason trialists in the 1950s, the PAC pass resisters in the 1960s, the Soweto youth in the 1970s, the ANC in the 1980s – were held in special cells, separated from other prisoners. Ironically, this allowed political prisoners to meet and talk in ways they could not do on the outside because of political suppression.

The visitors' room connected to the ATB was a place of profound emotion where those 'inside' could come into contact with their loved ones 'outside'. Separated from each other by a wall of wire mesh, prisoners remember the pleasure of visits but also the anguish of the long waits, the difficulties of screaming to one another over the noise of the room, and the farewells.

We were led down a clean, tarred road, flanked by beautifully manicured lawns and flower gardens, promising some paradise. But what kind? We went through a big iron gate to number 8 (the ATB) and were led up some stairs to section D. This D section was a big hall of a cell divided into numerous small cells of maybe two by two metres. They were made of diamond-mesh steel. They were called the *khulukhuthus* (isolation cells). I stayed a full three months in this hell.

Godfrey Moloi, My Life

NELSON MANDELA AND OTHER TREASON TRIALISTS ATTENDING COURT
Bailey's African History Archive

We stayed in the ATB for two weeks and despite the hardships our spirits remained extremely high. Our communal cell became a kind of convention for far-flung freedom fighters. Many of us had been living under severe restrictions, making it illegal for us to meet and talk. Now, our enemy had gathered us all under one roof for what became the largest and longest unbanned meeting of the Congress Alliance in years. Younger leaders met older leaders they had only read about. Men from Natal mingled with leaders from the Transvaal. We revelled in the opportunity to exchange ideas and experiences for two weeks while we awaited trial.

Nelson Mandela, Long Walk to Freedom

ROBERT SOBUKWE LEADING A PAN AFRICAN CONGRESS MARCH AGAINST THE PASS LAWS IN ORLANDO IN 1960 Bailey's African History Archive

My crime was being found without a night pass five minutes before midnight. In prison, I was kicked and thrashed every day. I saw many other prisoners being thrashed daily. All prisoners were called *Kaffir* at all times.

Henry Nxumalo, pass offender, Drum Magazine, 1954

PASS ARRESTS IN JOHANNESBURG *left and middle* Eli Weinberg - UWC Robben Island Museum, Mayibuye Archives, *right* Bailey's African History Archive

The Old Fort Prison Complex has become a dumping
ground for rubbish, a haven for vagrants, rats, a fire
hazard and a menace to public health, besides being an
eyesore. This potentially valuable historical monument
has literally been allowed to rot.

National Monuments Council document, SAHRA archives, March 1990

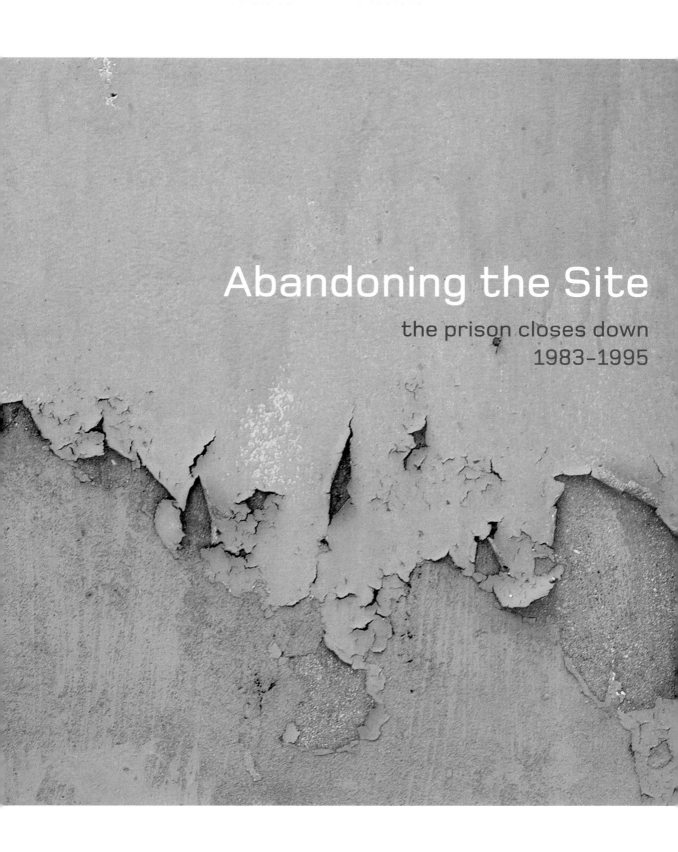

Abandoning the Site

the prison closes down
1983–1995

The Old Fort Finally Closes

On 31 January 1983, after nearly one hundred years, the Old Fort or Number Four, Johannesburg's notorious prison, closed down. Prisoners were moved to the newly built Diepkloof prison just outside Soweto. The City Council of Johannesburg leased the Fort to the Prisons Department to transform into a Prison Services Museum.

The 1904 Commission of Inquiry declared the Fort unfit, unsuitable for prisoners and incapable of being converted into a good prison. It never met prison standards in all of the years that it was in operation.

Flo Bird, former member of the National Monuments Council (NMC)

From the beginning, the Johannesburg City Council was concerned that the prison was situated too close to the civic centre on valuable land ripe for development. For years, they had planned for the prison to be removed to the outskirts of the city. But these plans never materialised. A modern prison was only built in 1983 and the Old Fort finally shut its doors.

Herbert Prins, heritage consultant

I was amongst the group of prisoners that they transferred from Number Four to the newly built Diepkloof prison. The new prison had individual cells, better food and clean blankets - unlike the blankets in Number Four that were washed once a year and filled with lice. So we named the new prison after a famous hotel of the time, Sun City.

Joe Thloloe, ex-political prisoner

WARDERS LEAVING THE OLD FORT 1983 MuseuMAfricA

The Abandoned Site

The Prisons Department's plans to transform the
Fort into a museum never materialised. After the
doors of the Fort closed, no maintenance was
carried out in any of the prison buildings. The site
quickly became derelict. Vandals began removing
brass fittings, ironmongery and other very valuable
items of historic importance. The Fort was neglected,
despite its status as a national monument.

The buildings had been ransacked.
You could buy the locks from the
cells on Louis Botha Avenue. They
were charging R1 000 a lock. An
enormous amount was sold out
of there.

Flo Bird, former member of the NMC

There was one occupant, a deaf
mute who set up home here.
He grew tomatoes in the little
courtyard next to Mandela's cell.
He fled whenever we came but we
used to see the drops of water
on the cement. I don't know what
happened to him.

Flo Bird, former member of the NMC

THE OLD FORT BECOMES A NATIONAL MONUMENT

The Old Fort was proclaimed a national monument on 27 November 1964 amidst a great deal of controversy. The Johannesburg City Council were wholly opposed as they believed that the only history attached to the Fort was 'slender and unimportant and after that its real history is that of notorious criminals and jail-breakers'. The Council had also hoped that the land would be made available for development and to build a park for overcrowded Hillbrow. But others considered the Old Fort to be Johannesburg's equivalent of Cape Town's Castle in its historical significance. They argued that the building was the most important remaining structure from the Zuid - Afrikaansche Republiek (ZAR). In the end, only the Fort and not the other prisons became a monument. The City Council was furious.

NUMBER FOUR – ABANDONED AND OVERGROWN *top* © David Goldblatt *bottom* Brian Orlin

Proposals

The future of the Fort became the subject of much speculation. The City Council received a host of proposals for a new function and use for the building, including turning the property into a nursery school and community centre for Hillbrow and even a hotel. In July 1990, seven years after the prison had closed, the Council called for formal submissions. The Council hoped that the site could be turned into a tourist venue similar to that of the Castle in Cape Town. The National Monuments Council (NMC), in charge of national heritage conservation in South Africa, were part of the discussions for a new tenant.

Two applications were submitted. One for a hotel and a complex of theatres, restaurant and community facilities. The other from the Transvaal Scottish Regiment to create its headquarters at the Fort as well as a museum on the history of the prison.

Herbert Prins, heritage consultant

We felt that a hotel would be an absolute insult to the place but we had to disguise our feelings about it politically. We couldn't refer to the political significance of the place, not even to our own committee. In the end, we were able to persuade the committee that the military presence of the Scottish Regiment was more in keeping with the site.

Flo Bird, former member of the NMC

CITY OF JOHANNESBURG

THE OLD FORT, HILLBROW: SUBMISSION OF PROPOSALS

The City Council of Johannesburg invites proposals for the use of the Fort. The Fort, which fronts onto Kotze Street, between Joubert Street Extension and Hospital Street, Hillbrow, dates back to the previous century when it was used as a fort by the Zuid-Afrikaansche Republiek and it has been declared a national monument. It later served as Johannesburg's Prison for many years but with the transfer of the prison to Meredale the Fort is now vacant.

The Fort, which is in urgent need of restoration and repair, lends itself to a number of excellent opportunities. In an atmosphere filled with history, innovative ideas of diverse nature can be implemented to the successful lessee's own benefit. Restaurants, curio shops, museums and offices are only a few of the many possibilities that can be exploited. The Council's view is that the Fort should remain open to the public as a place of interest and a tourist attraction, part of Johannesburg's turbulent early history, and for this reason is keen to receive proposals from persons wishing to hire or otherwise occupy the building on terms to be negotiated.

The Council is anxious that the historical character of the building should be maintained, much in the same way as the Castle in Cape Town has been developed as a museum to the country's military and penal history. The buildings, as stated, are in need of repair and it will be the successful applicant's responsibility to do all repair and restoration work to the satisfaction of both the Council and the National Monuments Council.

Written proposals indicating the type of lease or other occupational arrangement envisaged by the applicant, the duration thereof, the improvements contemplated by the applicant and evidence of his means to carry them out, should be submitted to the City Secretary, PO Box 1049, Johannesburg, 2000, or the Civic Centre, Braamfontein, by not later than 17th August 1990 and should be accompanied by explanatory drawings and plans. Working drawings are not required at this stage. Arrangements can be made to inspect the Fort during normal business hours by telephoning Mr F Wolff (011) 407-7360).

H T VEALE
City Secretary

5552790

THE NATIONAL MONUMENTS COUNCIL

The National Monuments Council was the statutory heritage organisation, responsible for the administration of the National Monuments Act, 1969. In terms of this legislation, the destruction of a declared monument or any part thereof was prohibited and buildings over 50 years old were also protected against unauthorised alterations and demolitions. The NMC was replaced by the South African Heritage Resource Agency (SAHRA) in 2000 in accordance with the South African Heritage Resource Act (Act 25 of 1999). SAHRA's vision was to provide for the identification, conservation, protection and promotion of heritage – tangible and intangible – for present and future generations.

The Transvaal Scottish Regiment and the Fort Foundation

The Transvaal Scottish under the command of Commandant Spike Becker, had set up a specific agency, the Fort Foundation, to acquire the Fort premises. The Foundation submitted plans to the Council for considerable internal alterations as well as the demolition of some of the hospital sections within the Fort. The regiment needed the space for a parade ground. Initially, the City Council and the National Monuments Council (NMC) were reluctant to approve the demolition.

While the Fort Foundation fully understands the delicate nature of this site and also understands the concerns of the NMC about the Fort, it is also important to remember that the Fort is rapidly deteriorating. The constant weathering of the site is causing untold damage and should the Fort be left for another year it will become structurally unsafe and might have to be destroyed in total leaving very little or no record of what is presently there.

Spike Becker, Commandant of the Scottish Regiment and member of the Fort Foundation, SAHRA Archive, November 1990

Our choice at that time was a huge demolition, including the buildings where the mentally ill and people with infectious diseases were kept and where prisoners were whipped, or to lose a lot more if we agreed to a hotel. We persuaded the Council to give the Regiment permission for the demolitions.

Flo Bird, former member of the NMC

THE TRANSVAAL SCOTTISH REGIMENT

The Transvaal Scottish Regiment was established in 1902 after the conclusion of the South African War (Anglo-Boer War). The founding members were volunteers who had been part of a Scottish unit that had demobilised and remained in the colony. The regiment is now part of the South African National Defence Force. Members all have civilian occupations but are required to be far more than mere reservists as the unit is one of the main striking forces of the country's army.

THE HOSPITAL SECTION OF THE OLD FORT THAT WAS DEMOLISHED BY THE FORT FOUNDATION TO MAKE SPACE FOR A PARADE GROUND Chris Reilly

A Living Museum

The Fort Foundation had ambitious plans. Besides being the headquarters for the regiment, they wanted to create a living museum of military and penal history. The restoration project was launched on 6 July, 1991 in impressive military style. The skirling of a lone bagpiper on the parapets was followed by a parade of pipers and drums. Alderman Eliot Kretzmer, the mayor of Johannesburg, pledged a R2 million short-term loan towards the restoration of the Fort. The Foundation set out to look for more money to turn their ideas into reality but within a year their dreams were scuppered.

Our mission is to restore the Fort and maintain it. I dream of processions, military tattoos and the enjoyment of the public in historic events.

Spike Becker, Commandant of the Scottish Regiment and member of the Fort Foundation, Rosebank Killarney Gazette, July 1991

We are looking to our major companies to help fulfil this exciting project – a museum within one of the few remaining earth forts – Johannesburg's Fort. It will be a fantastic tourist attraction.

Rae Graham, member of the Fort Foundation, Rosebank Killarney Gazette, 2 July 1991

The first phase of the project for the Regiment's headquarters was completed. But the further renovations for the tourist facilities never went ahead. The Foundation were unable to raise sufficient funds from the JCC or anywhere else.

Herbert Prins, heritage consultant

One questions why the City Fathers who saw good to invest millions in a new Civic Theatre – a building whose interior will never be 'graced' by the majority of the inhabitants of the greater metropolitan area – have not contributed financially towards the creation of a low-key, accessible, 'people's museum'. This project, whose costs represent a fraction of those invested in the former grandiose institution, could possibly be halted in its tracks. Further deterioration of the remaining structures would inevitably result and the first phase would lose its viability. We would have failed to take an opportunity toenhance an already rich and diverse urban fabric…

Extract from 'Plans', July 1992

IMAGES TAKEN OF THE OLD FORT IN 1991 BEFORE THE PLANNED RESTORATION PROJECT Chris Reilly

Out with the Regiment, In with the Infantry

The rental agreement between the Scottish Regiment and the City Council also fell through and the regiment did not move into their newly renovated headquarters. The Council took back the control of the Fort premises from the Fort Foundation. Once again, Council was without a tenant and the site was wholly abandoned. A Fort Steering Committee was set up by the Council to re-examine the use of the Fort.

The Council faced the problem of either going back to a proposal call again or finding another tenant. At this time, the Council faced another issue. The Rand Light Infantry (RLI) - a senior infantry regiment - had the title to the Union Grounds in Twist Street and had occupied the Grounds since 1945. The Council wanted this land for a taxi rank. They requested that the RLI give up the building and come to the Fort.

Flo Bird, former member of the NMC

The Regiment agreed to move into the Old Fort even though it was not in an ideal state. Once the Regiment took occupation officially on 26 April 1993 the buildings were secured, vagrants removed and repairs and maintenance commenced. We managed the Old Fort until 2004. We ensured that the Old Fort was accessible under supervision to the many historians, students, dignitaries and heads of state that visited the monument through its occupation. Many scenes from international and local movies were shot at the Fort, including *Gandhi*. In keeping with our civic duties, we played an important and valuable role in managing this highly sensitive site during a country going through transformation.

Lt Col Selwyn Vos MMM, JCD, Chairman of the RLI Regimental Council

Under the auspices of the Regiment, the Reserve Force Council had their headquarters at the Old Fort, as did the 'Moths' and numerous affiliate organisations.

Lt Col Selwyn Vos MMM, JCD, Chairman of the RLI Regimental Council

The Old Fort was at least being looked after by the RLI. Number Four was going to rack and ruin.

Brian Orlin, development manager, Constitution Hill

↘

THE RAND LIGHT INFANTRY

The Rand Light Infantry is one of South Africa's senior infantry regiments. It was established in 1905 and was first known as the Transvaal Cycle and Motor Corps. After the South African War (Anglo-Boer War), Britain was anxious to reduce her costly garrison troops in South Africa and she encouraged the establishment of local units of volunteers to replace British soldiers. Several regiments emerged. In 1913, the corps became known as the Rand Light Infantry (RLI).

'The Regiment has military, civic and international duties, is apolitical and It is called on to serve the government of the day. The City of Johannesburg bestowed the Freedom of The City on the Regiment in 1955 and it has served the City through the industrial strike of 1914 and the Rand Revolt of 1922. The Regiment served the Country through two World Wars and in South West Africa from 1976-1990, the 1994 election. From the Regimental Headquarters at the Old Fort, we had a contingency plan in place in the event of disaster management and many volunteers in the Regiment served at each and every voting station. The RLI is presently in the Democratic Republic Of Congo.'

Lt Col Selwyn Vos MMM, JCD, Chairman of the RLI Regimental Council

The Johannesburg Security Department

While the Rand Light Infantry took care of the Old Fort, more sinister developments had been taking place in other parts of the site. In 1988, the Security Department of the Johannesburg City Council took occupation of the Women's Jail and sections of the Awaiting Trial Block and Number Four. Some members of the Security Department were also members of the infamous Civil Co-operation Bureau (CCB), a military intelligence structure involved in dirty tricks against anti-apartheid activists. The CCB was also responsible for several high-profile assassinations. They had an arsenal of weapons stored in the isolation cells of the Women's Jail.

As a Joburg ratepayer, we thought that the traffic department and the security department had guards who looked after cemeteries and the parks. I'm not sure that the Councillors knew about the CCB. I've never asked a ward Councillor, 'Are you aware that we own a whole fleet of bloody Saracens? But that was quite horrific for me. Remember, I was a very active ratepayer and I had never seen any mention of buying the latest Saracen in my Council Agenda. There was quite a lot of evil about it.

Flo Bird, former member of the NMC

My first reaction when I saw that the Women's Jail was occupied by the Security Department was, 'Wow! What an unbelievable sight! And what a bloody waste to have the security people in what is obviously a central part of the history of the city and of the country.' They had given no thought or respect to what had happened here. Some of the traffic cops who had impounded vehicles had a chop shop (a place where stolen cars are broken up for parts) going in Number Four.

Neil Fraser, former executive director, Central Johannesburg Partnership

THE DOORS OF THE ISOLATION CELLS IN THE WOMEN'S JAIL WHERE THE SECURITY DEPARTMENT STORED THEIR WEAPONS Andrew Meintjes

THE ARSENAL VAULT THAT WAS INSTALLED BY THE JOHANNESBURG SECURITY DEPARTMENT TO PROTECT THE ISOLATION CELLS Guto Bussab

The Old Fort was the Robben Island of Johannnesburg. A
new Constitutional Court rising there would dramatise the
transformation of South Africa from a racist, authoritarian society
to a constitutional democracy. A more South African centre of
repression and hope could not have been found. Above all, it had
history. This wasn't just a neutral space – this was a space of intense
drama, of human emotion, of repression, of resistance. And here was
the chance to convert negativity into positivity.

Albie Sachs, Constitutional Court judge

Finding a Home

the constitutional court
needs a new building
1995–1996

New Beginnings

While the high walls of the Fort hid and enclosed the sinister and the forgotten, huge changes were afoot in South Africa. The Convention for a Democratic South Africa (CODESA) set out to write a new constitution for the country. After days and nights of negotiations, multiple deadlocks and breakthroughs, an interim constitution was adopted in November 1993. In April 1994, the first democratic elections ushered in a new era.

Just less than a year after the elections, President Nelson Mandela inaugurated South Africa's first Constitutional Court on 14 February 1995. This institution was established to defend the democratic principles and values of the new constitutional order. Mandela nominated Arthur Chaskalson as the first president of the court. Another four judges were appointed from the ranks of the Supreme Court while a Judicial Services Commission appointed the remaining six judges. The judges heard their first case on 15 February 1995.

Yvonne Mokgoro, Constitutional Court judge

CYRIL RAMAPHOSA WITH PRESIDENT NELSON MANDELA, 7 MAY 1996, JUST AFTER PARLIAMENT
HAD UNANIMOUSLY VOTED IN FAVOUR OF THE NEW CONSTITUTION Picturenet Africa

The last time I appeared in court was to hear whether or not I was going to be sentenced to death. Fortunately, for myself and my colleagues, we were not. Today I rise not as an accused, but on behalf of the people of South Africa, to inaugurate a court South Africa has never had, a court on which hinges the future of our democracy.

Nelson Mandela, Constitutional Court inauguration, 14 February 1995

PRESIDENT NELSON MANDELA AND CHIEF JUSTICE ARTHUR CHASKALSON UNVEILING THE NEW COURT LOGO AT THE INAUGURATION OF THE CONSTITUTIONAL COURT
Raymond Preston, Picturenet

THE NEW LOGO OF THE CONSTITUTIONAL COURT

The tree was central to the design of the logo. There are eleven branches that represent the different languages and the eleven judges. At the top, are four branches suggesting the shape of the South African coastline. The South African flag is also subtly suggested by the Y-shape in the tree trunk. There are eleven people under the tree in an integration of both positive and negative shapes: both black and white elements interrelating. The design incorporates a multitude of faceted pieces that together form a circular whole. The circle is not bound all around. Some of the facets extend beyond its edges. This was an important element to release a dynamic energy, to show the court's progressiveness and the energy of the judges, their intense passion.

Carolyn Parton, designer, 2005

THE CONSTITUTIONAL COURT OF SOUTH AFRICA

When the Court was established, we had nothing. There was one chair when Arthur Chaskalson interviewed potential secretaries. That's all the court had, one chair. We had temporary office space, a building with long bland corridors. The huge advantage was that we could invent ourselves. We couldn't bear the old coat of arms. It was associated with death sentences, banning orders and all the commands of a racist authoritarian government. The idea of the mail of the court going out under that imprimatur was emotionally untenable. We wanted a new logo.

Albie Sachs, Constitutional Court judge

A New Building for the New Court

The new logo for the Constitutional Court established the idea of a court that would have its own character – a character that was African and that represented the diversity of the South African people. The new logo was also the beginning of a much larger project – to build a new building for the new court. This was to be South Africa's first national post-apartheid government building.

The dramatic change in South Africa was not from white to black, but from the rule of men to the rule of law. It was a natural consequence that it was the Constitution that was going to be the prevailing power in the new South Africa. It followed that the body that was the protector of the Constitution - the Constitutional Court - should be recognised by a building of commensurate importance.

Johann Kriegler, former Constitutional Court judge

Our accommodation in Braampark was temporary, but we couldn't postpone dispensing constitutional justice until we had our own building. I remember at the luncheon after the inauguration of the Court in February 1995, Arthur mentioned that we would need a building of our own. I think that was the first public mention of it.

Albie Sachs, Constitutional Court judge

This is a young country. People feel deeply and passions swirl. The Constitutional Court, possibly more than any other institution, stands for, defends and symbolises the integrity of our nation and the fundamental rights of all our citizens. We want a place that will reflect the importance with which people view this court, the role it plays in their lives and its function of ensuring that the Constitution is sovereign.

Pius Langa, Deputy Chief Justice, Sunday Times, 21 March 2004

Choosing a Site

The first task of the Department of Public Works – who were responsible for building the new Constitutional Court – was to work with the City Council to find a suitable site in Johannesburg. The court was a prestigious tenant and many interest groups vied to attract the court.

We were wooed by many people who tried to persuade us to build the Constitutional Court on their site. We visited Crown Mines, the old synagogue in Wolmarans Street, and down near Anglo American where De Beers is, and the Johannnesburg Technikon.

Johann Kriegler, former Constitutional Court judge

The Wolmarans Street shul is a fascinating building, but it didn't breathe. The independence of the court required that it had its own space, that it should not be too crowded in by the city. We were also referred to the old post office. It's a marvellous old building, but again it's crowded in by the city.

Albie Sachs, Constitutional Court judge

We were shown the Pieter Roos Park where the court would be in a slightly more contemplative setting than at the inner city sites. But there are so few green spaces in Johannesbug that I was opposed to the idea of diminishing public open spaces.

Kate O'Regan, Constitutional Court judge

We had a very interesting visit to Midrand. We were given a very intelligent and thoughtful presentation, but it just seemed all wrong. Contemporary style high-tech buildings, and it would have represented cosiness with business.

Albie Sachs, Constitutional Court judge

I was looking at all of these sites with only half an eye because I knew where we were going.

Johann Kriegler, former Constitutional Court judge

Visiting Number Four

One of the sites suggested by the Johannesburg City Council was the Old Fort, parts of which were occupied at the time by the Rand Light Infantry and the Johannesburg Security Department. The judges visited the site as a group.

I have known this site for donkey's years. When I was still practising at the bar, I used to come and see clients in the Old Fort. Also, I'm a Joburg freak, and I went to the Fort after the Prisons Department had abandoned it on more than one occasion. I felt like a little boy - there was something adventurous about coming to this abandoned place.

Johann Kriegler, former Constitutional Court judge

Some of us had personal associations with the suffering that was experienced at this place. I mean, my father was jailed here for pass law offences when I was very young. I was born and I grew up in Kimberley and as happens in most black families, parents go out to Joburg to find work and we were left with our grandmother. My father was arrested and he sat for about six months at the Fort.

Yvonne Mokgoro, Constitutional Court judge

It was strange country for me. I'd never been there. I hadn't interviewed clients there. I hadn't been locked up there but in Cape Town. I'd only known about it through stories of others. It had a totally ruined, derelict character. But it was the site's potential for renovation and resurrection that was so captivating. My heart just flipped, because the chance of turning things around, which we've done with our country, was so intense and powerful.

Albie Sachs, Constitutional Court judge

I recall wading our way through long grass and blackjacks and rubble all over the place, and having a look and realising that indeed it would be a remarkable site for the court, even though it did look a bit like a rubbish dump at the time.

Kate O'Regan, Constitutional Court judge

THE JUDGES OF THE CONSTITUTIONAL COURT OUTSIDE THE ISOLATION CELLS OF NUMBER FOUR. AMONGST THE GROUP OF JUDGES ARE RICHARD GOLDSTONE, ZAK YAKOOB, ALBIE SACHS, ARTHUR CHASKALSON, SANDILE NGCOBO, JOHANN KRIEGLER AND THOLE MADALA *Mariola Biela, The Citizen*

The Hidden Attractions

Through the weeds, the rubble and the ruins, the judges could see the potential of the prison site. Its location in the inner city, the views it commanded over Johannesburg and most importantly, the history of the prisons were all compelling reasons for the judges to locate the court at Number Four.

VIEW OF HILLBROW FROM THE RAMPARTS Chris Reilly

The location cheek by jowl with Hillbrow was
a drawcard rather than a detractor. We were
particularly concerned about not having a remote,
alien place. To place the Constitutional Court
where it was accessible was a non-negotiable.

Johann Kriegler, former Constitutional Court judge

The other wonderful thing
was that it is both looked
upon and commands a view,
which seemed appropriate
for a court like this.

Kate O'Regan, Constitutional Court judge

I was very excited about converting
this place, not just physically, but
emotionally too into a place that
protected human rights. The site would
urge us not to forget what happened in
the past. The bricks would be there as
reminders that this is a route that we
never, never want to take again.

Yvonne Mokgoro, Constitutional Court judge

We felt excited by the symbolism of the old
prisons, whose function had once been so
oppressive, becoming, under the Constitution, a
place representing freedom and human rights.

*Pius Langa, Deputy Chief Justice, Sunday Times,
21 March 2004*

Albie and I were always for this site.
We had very little difficulty persuading
our colleagues.

Johann Kriegler, former Constitutional Court judge

Johannesburg PH2003/885

THE PRISON COMPLEX IN 1957 SURROUNDED BY THE HIGH-RISE BUILDINGS OF HILLBROW MuseuMAfricA

A Difficult Decision

Together with two advisory architects, Vivien and Derek Japha, the judges identified the position for the court at the highest point on the northern slope of the site. But they were faced with a dilemma. The Awaiting Trial Block (ATB) prison was in the way. The prison was symbolic of the very nature of the jail – black men and women repeatedly being arrested and criminalised because of the colour of their skin. The prison had, over the years, also housed waves of political prisoners including the treason trialists in 1956 and PAC anti-pass protesters led by Sobukwe 1960. Passions and principles came to the surface in a debate about whether or not the ATB could be demolished.

One day, Derek Japha and I walked over to the site. He said he thought it was a wonderful site for a new building. It's got space. It's got slope. It's connected with the urban fabric, but not dominated by it. He was very inspired. But he said if you kept the ATB, the Court would be overshadowed by it. It wouldn't have any space. The prison would have to go.

Albie Sachs, Constitutional Court judge

The National Monuments Council was immediately up in arms. They thought we were going to destroy a national heritage site. I came back with a fairly pungent response: 'You heritage people have got a temerity to talk about us wanting to destroy it. You're allowing it to go to rack and ruin. When last did any of you go and have a look at it? Ceilings are being taken out and hobos are occupying it.

Johann Kriegler, former Constitutional Court judge

The Monuments Council and its successors have always had a terrible problem: the legislation provides for all kinds of strong preservation measures, but neither now, nor in the past, have there been the necessary funds from government to make it possible for the Council to carry out their preservation functions properly.

Herbert Prins, heritage consultant

It was nature that was pulling down buildings and yet the idea of any intervention on the site provoked almost automatic protectiveness of what was actually being ruined.

Albie Sachs, Constitutional Court judge

THE AWAITING TRIAL BLOCK AFTER THE PRISON HAD CLOSED. THE IMAGE ON THE BOTTOM RIGHT IS OF ONE OF THE BARRED WINDOWS OF THE VISITOR CENTRE THROUGH WHICH VISITORS COMMUNICATED WITH PRISONERS © David Goldblatt

Negotiations

A decision had to be made. The National Monuments Council (NMC) wanted the court on site but they strongly opposed the demolition of the Awaiting Trial Block (ATB). The judges stood firm.

When the Monuments Council said to the judges, 'We love the idea that you build your Court here, but we think you should keep the ATB,' this fell to some extent on deaf ears. It came to a point where there was an impasse between the judges and the Monuments Council. The judges said, 'Look, this is where the court should go. And if we can't build our court there, then we will have to look somewhere else for a site.

Herbert Prins, heritage consultant

In considering the value of the buildings, not only architectural criteria should be featured. If the social history is to be fathomed, then physical manifestations are important.

NMCI, SAHRA archives, March 1997

There was a hell of a fight. I was absolutely horrified, because we felt that the ATB was tremendously important. And of course the City Council and the Central Johannnesburg Partnership were leaning very heavily on the Monuments Council to give the Court permission to knock it down.

Flo Bird, former member of the NMC

Quite frankly, I am not a great fan of prisons and I don't feel this huge regret when prisons are razed to the ground. What was it going to be used for, a rather ugly, 1940s building, in which people had suffered enormously, very often unjustly? That something can rise, phoenix-like from the ashes, which is the antidote to it, seems to me to be a powerful message of possibility for transformation in South Africa. I suppose it's very difficult to get everybody to agree.

Kate O'Regan, Constitutional Court judge

The Decision is Made

A decision was eventually made in early 1997. The NMC gave way to the judges'
request that the ATB be demolished to make way for the new court. As part
of the agreement, the NMC insisted that the building be commemorated as
part of the new developments.

There was really no alternative but to give
permission to demolish the ATB. The Court
presented us with an incredible opportunity to
take care of the site. This decision has been very
seriously criticised by many people, particularly ex-
prisoners, who feel that that particular building had
a very important place.

Herbert Prins, heritage consultant

Consensus was reached with the heritage
representatives that we could use the
site but would make as little an inroad as
possible into the other prison buildings.
The thought that the Fort was going to be
preserved and that Number Four was going
to be preserved was a wonderful relief.

Johann Kriegler, former Constitutional Court judge

I am happy to have been the mayor at the
time the Council agreed. I pushed to put the
Constitutional Court there, as this is a victory
for the people who once were in the prison.
It is a way of honouring their part in the
struggle for liberation.

*Isaac Mogase, ex-prisoner and former Mayor of
Johannnesburg*

WALL TEXTURE OF THE FORT COURTYARD Andrew Meintjes

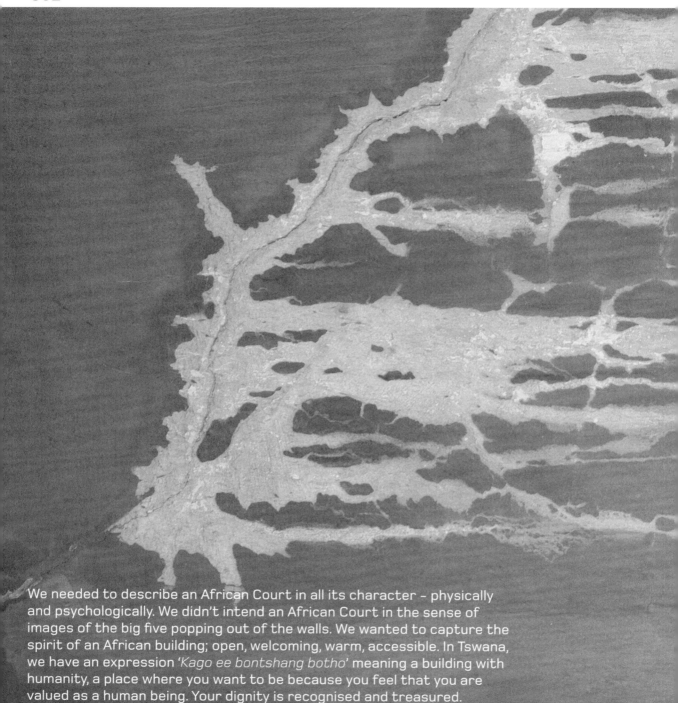

We needed to describe an African Court in all its character – physically and psychologically. We didn't intend an African Court in the sense of images of the big five popping out of the walls. We wanted to capture the spirit of an African building; open, welcoming, warm, accessible. In Tswana, we have an expression *'Kago ee bontshang botho'* meaning a building with humanity, a place where you want to be because you feel that you are valued as a human being. Your dignity is recognised and treasured.

Yvonne Mokgoro, Constitutional Court judge

Imagining the Court

setting the design brief
1997-1998

A New Approach for a New Institution

Public buildings in South Africa are usually designed in-house by the Department of Public Works (DPW) or by DPW-appointed architects. The DPW is the client, finds the funding for construction and determines all the building specifications. The judges felt, however, that the new court should reflect the excitement and optimism about a new accessible system of justice that the new constitution brought with it, and they decided that a competition would be the best way to break with the intimidating and derivative public architecture of the past.

When government hands out work to its favourites, the favourites produce what they think government wants. For the sake of good architecture you need competitions. That's how you get fresh ideas and innovation.

Albie Sachs, Constitutional Court judge

This is the first architectural competition which has been approved by government as an alternative way for the state to engage in the design of important sites that reflect our legacy.

Jeff Radebe, Minister of Public Works, Competition Brief preface, 1996

There had been derision within the architectural community about some of the hideous crypto-fascist public buildings put up over the last few decades. So we grabbed at the idea of a competition with both hands. It is a new way of ensuring that we get the best and by carefully structuring the competition, we encourage emerging architects.

Ian Phillips, special adviser to Jeff Radebe, The Star, 26 October 1997

THE JOHANNESBURG SUPREME COURT, THE JOHANNESBURG MAGISTRATE'S COURT, THE PALACE OF JUSTICE IN PRETORIA

The Site

IMAGES OF THE SITE AS THEY APPEARED IN THE COMPETITION BRIEF FOR THE CONSTITUTIONAL COURT Athol Franz Studio

Trusting Our Imaginations

A diverse set of skills and political acumen was needed for the job of drawing up the competition brief. A number of interested parties got involved, including the Department of Justice, which was putting up the money; the Department of Public Works, which was responsible for public buildings; the Johannnesburg Metropolitan Council, which owned the land and was interested in the development of the court; the National Monuments Council, which was concerned about what was going to happen to heritage buildings; and, of course, the judges themselves.

Why were the judges themselves so involved in the building project? I never thought of it as anything but a public trust. We are the Constitutional Court; we are establishing a monument; it has got to be worthy of that trust that has been given to us. All human beings - let me say all males - are ego-driven. The thought that we could contribute to something concrete, something for the ages, was very exciting. We were destiny aware. We were making jurisprudence and a building to go with it.

Johann Kriegler, former Constitutional Court judge

Architects generally have no or very little experience regarding the functioning of courts. Courts present particular problems of their own.

Laurie Ackermann, former Constitutional Court judge, memorandum to Judge Sachs, 1996

We could have followed precedent and tradition in the way lawyers do. We could have taken a little bit of this building and a little bit of that building. Some people feel comforted by that. They feel that's a real court. It looks like a real court. It represents the power of the state. If a building like that has any visual symbols inside, they'll also be borrowed: the blindfolded woman with the scales of justice from Greek mythology, or Roman columns. That's a distrust of Africa, of our own imaginations.

Albie Sachs, Constitutional Court judge

competition

FOR THE NEW
CONSTITUTIONAL
COURT BUILDING
OF SOUTH AFRICA

PROMOTED BY
THE DEPARTMENT OF PUBLIC WORKS

As South Africa transforms its systems of governance, appropriate architectural expressions are required to reflect new democratic institutions and profound changes in society and culture. The competition for the design of the Constitutional Court building — the first major public structure of the new constitutional order — provides an ideal opportunity to meet this challenge. The site is the Old Fort precinct in Johannesburg, an area with a rich but grim history as a prison compound where many political prisoners were detained. This entire precinct will be developed as "Constitution Hill", which will become a public space for the city and a symbolic place for the nation, where the Court and human rights institutions will be accommodated alongside museums in the historic prison buildings. The competition will focus on the new building for the Court, but competitors will also be asked for proposals to make the entire site an appropriate setting for all these new uses.

■ THE COMPETITION
The competition will be conducted in two stages. The first stage will require only sufficient work to enable the jury to select between three and five finalists, who will develop their designs in the second stage. Anonymity will be preserved during both stages of the competition.

■ WHO CAN ENTER
Although aimed primarily at architects and other professionals involved with the built environment, the competition is open to any person who wishes to enter. Approval for the competition to be open has been obtained from the Minister of Public Works.

■ THE JURY
The jury for both stages of the competition will be as follows:
The President of the Constitutional Court, Justice Arthur Chaskalson, or his nominee;
The Mayor of Greater Johannesburg, Councillor Isaac Mogase;
Geoffrey Bawa, architect, Sri Lanka;
Charles Correa, architect, India;
Gerard Damstra, architect, Department of Public Works;
Peter Davey, Editor, *Architectural Review*;
Willie Meyer, architect nominated by the SABTACO, SACA and SAIA;
Tenjiwe Mtintso, Chairperson, SA Gender Commission;
Herbert Prins, architect nominated by the SA National Monuments Council.

■ AWARDS TO FINALISTS
An award of R60 000 will be made to each finalist to defray the cost of preparing bona fide second stage entries.

■ THE FIRST PRIZE
Subject to Treasury approval, the winner will be commissioned to execute the project at the published scale of fees for design, contract administration and inspection.

■ KEY DATES (Local time)
Final date for registration:	25/8/97
First stage submission:	6/11/97
Commencement of the second stage:	24/11/97
Second stage submission:	12/02/97

■ SITE VISITS
Competitors wishing to visit the site may make arrangements through the Registrar: fax number ++27 12 325 8095.

■ REGISTRATION FEE
The registration fee is SAR50 for citizens and residents of South Africa and SADC countries and US$50 for all other entrants.

HOW TO REGISTER

1. Pay the registration fee. In South Africa or a SADC country, pay in rands. In other countries, pay in US dollars. In South Africa, deposit the fee into the account given below. In other countries, arrange a swift (telegraphic) transfer into the account given below.

Account name	Architectural Competition, New Constitutional Court;
Bank	Trust Bank, a Division of ABSA Bank;
Branch	Peyntons;
Swift Code	ABSAZAJJ
Bank Code	51 59 4500
Account Number	90 5111 4358.

2. Send notification providing the following: proof of payment of registration fee; name; address; telephone number; and fax number. Unless all of these are provided, you cannot be registered. Where applicable, also give your professional status and affiliation. This should be sent by post or fax to the address or numbers given below.

By Post: The Registrar, Architectural Competition, New Constitutional Court, Department of Public Works, Private Bag X65, Pretoria 0001, South Africa.
By Fax: Addressed as above to numbers ++27 12 325 8095 or 323 8509.

Registered competitors will be sent the brief and conditions.

CTP BOOK PRINTERS, CAPE   ALICE BARRY GRAPHICS

THE COVER OF THE CONSTITUTIONAL COURT COMPETITION BOOKLET

The Design Brief

The Department of Public Works (DPW) agreed to waive
its space specifications for the new building. Architects,
government officials, heritage experts and the judges debated
and decided on issues ranging from the detailed specifications
for the court chamber to personal ablution facilities.

Of all the drafting I've done in my life, including
helping draft sections of the Constitution, this
must have been amongst the most delicate and
interesting. We spent months on the brief, both on
getting the text and the specifications right. But
the key thing wasn't the accommodation, that was
straightforward. The difficult thing was describing
the character of the building.

Albie Sachs, Constitutional Court judge

We made some important interventions. The DPW states that
judges are entitled to piddle privately. People of our position are
entitled to private facilities. We traded in that privilege for extra
space in our chambers. I don't think that we should see the future
of the building through a sewerage pipe. Having communal toilets is
more sensible for plumbing purposes than having private ones.

Johann Kriegler, former Constitutional Court judge

The building must be rooted in the South African landscape, both physically and culturally.

It should not overemphasise the symbols or vernacular expressions of any section of the population, nor be a pastiche of them all.

It should weather gracefully and be made of material which is enduring.

It must be restrained, simple and elegant rather than opulent, garish or ornate.

It should have a distinctive presence, as befits its unique role and should convey an atmosphere of balance, rationality, security, tranquillity and humanity.

It should be dignified and serious, but it should have a welcoming, open and attractive character and make everyone feel free to enter and safe and protected once inside.

Extracts from the brief reproduced in the original form

The Rules of the Competition

The nature of the competition itself also came under scrutiny. After much debate, the judges and Department of Public Works (DPW) decided to go for an international, two-stage competition. The first stage required submissions on the key concepts for the Constitutional Court and for the development of the site as a whole. The second stage would involve five finalists who would submit detailed design proposals for the Court and the environs. Non-architects were encouraged to participate because there were very few trained black architects in South Africa at that time. All entrants would be anonymous.

Spurred on by the democratic experience of the Constitutional Assembly, which brought all of our people into the task of writing our new democratic Constitution, we insisted that we must ensure that as many people who wished to make a contribution to the design of the Constitutional Court should do so, regardless of whether they are qualified architects or not.

Jeff Radebe, Minister of Public Works, speech on the occasion of announcing the winner of the Constitutional Court Architectural Competition, April 1998

The competition was structured so that anyone could put forward their vision for the site.

Vivien Japha, vice-president of the South African Institute of Architects

I motivated very strongly for national competition. I said, 'It's our Constitution; it's our history. We've got architects. We can do it.' But Laurie Ackermann said, 'Go for an international competition. If South African architects are the best, then they'll win.'

Albie Sachs, Constitutional Court judge

The Jury

Eight people representing the various interest groups, were selected for the jury. Albie Sachs represented the court, and Herbert Prins, the Monuments Council. Isaac Mogase, an ex-prisoner and the mayor of Johannesburg from 1994 until 2000, represented the local council, and Gerard Damstra, also an architect, the DPW. Willie Meyer represented the South African architectural profession. Three major international architecture figures made up the rest of the jury: Charles Correa of India, Geoffrey Bawa of Sri Lanka and Peter Davey, UK-based editor of *Architectural Review*. Thenjiwe Mtintso, also an ex-prisoner and chair of the Commission on Gender Equality, was approached when it became apparent that there were no women on the jury.

Thenji at first was saying 'What the hell am I doing here? You saw you didn't have a woman and you appointed me.' And she was absolutely right. But from then onwards she was the most influential member of the jury and these three top-notch international expert architects were dazzled by her.

Albie Sachs, Constitutional Court judge

In that room I brought in my own particular expertise - a freedom fighter, an African woman, a former detainee of the notorious women's prison. I asked myself what the building should say to women. I took what I knew from my late mother, a poor black woman who grew up in the rural areas and migrated to the informal settlements of Joburg. She would say that these places scare the hell out of you. 'They are ugly, heavy and austere.' She knew, because she was regularly arrested for the dompas. This court needed to be for the people, unlike anything of the old order.

Thenjiwe Mtintso, Commission on Gender Equality

I was detained at Number Four on a number of occasions, the first time in 1957 when I was arrested for a pass offence. That was not the last time. My wife, a nursing sister, had to struggle to keep the home going. Two of my children were in tertiary education and graduated while I was in detention. I was obviously very excited to now be a member of the jury. If I had told the warders that one day I would be mayor of Johannesburg and on the jury to select a new Constitutional Court building, they would have killed me.

Isaac Mogase, ex-prisoner and former mayor of Johannnesburg

More Than Just Freedom

Just prior to the competition brief going out, the National Monuments Council (NMC) managed to have the whole site declared a national monument. In 1964, only the Old Fort had been declared a national monument. But from then on, any changes to any of the heritage buildings on site would be subject to NMC approval. The very last decision that was made before the competition brief went out, was what the site would be called.

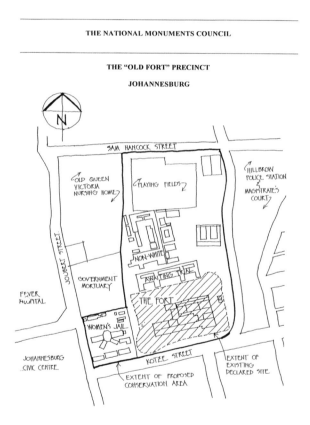

The intention of the declaration is to protect the cultural significance of the property. The NMC commits itself to the commissioning of comprehensive conservation survey of the to-be-declared complexes of buildings...to better understand the precinct's heritage dynamic, both tangible and intangible.

JJ Bruwer, Manager Northern Region, NMC, SAHRA archives, 16 September 1998

MAP OF THE HERITAGE AREA PROPOSED TO BECOME A NATIONAL MONUMENT

The question of a name for the precinct arose. I remember, we had a meeting of the judges and I proposed that the whole area be called 'Freedom Hill' and that it be dedicated to freedom. Chief Justice Arthur Chaskalson responded with 'Constitution Hill'. I was a little dubious; I thought that was giving a kind of a legal slant to the place. But I'm very pleased that he made that suggestion. The word freedom is everywhere. You have 'Freedom Square' and 'Freedom Park', freedom this and freedom that. 'Constitution Hill' is much more specific and it gives it a very distinctive character. From then on we referred to the development as 'Constitution Hill'.

Albie Sachs, Constitutional Court judge

The Launch of the Competition

The competition was launched on 15 April 1997 at a formal ceremony in the Women's Jail. During the ceremony, a partnership declaration was signed between the parties who were to be involved in the building of the court.

The task of designing a complex befitting the rich, complex legacy of this site is a task that deserves the greatest amount of public participation as possible. We would like to foster a greater culture of excellence and sensitivity among architects and other professionals involved in the built environment. We need to encourage the development of regional appropriate architectural forms. Such projects should acknowledge local human needs and social values; recognise a symbiosis between natural and cultural/historical landscapes, with an appreciation of climatic and environmental factors; excellence with limited means; assert the interaction of technology and local labour resources; and promote the ultimate inspiration of innovation.

The Architectural Competition we are launching today arises out of this commitment. This is the first such competition which has been approved by government as an alternative way for the state to engage in the design of important sites that reflect our legacy.

Jeff Radebe, Minister of Public Works, speech at the competition launch, 1997

Responses

The competition attracted an unexpected amount of interest, both locally and abroad.

Five hundred and sixty architects and non-architects with a vision of what the Old Fort could become are working to meet the deadline of November 6 for the first phase of the competition. Few would have expected the unusual strength of local and international interest. Clearly, South Africa's transition to democracy still causes international astonishment.

Carmel Rickard, Sunday Times, 26 October, 1997

The esteem in which our Constitutional Court is held, both by ourselves and in the international community, is aptly demonstrated by the interest which this competition attracted from across the world. In the international participants in this process, whether in the competition or in the adjudication, we see the living reality of solidarity in struggle transformed into partnership for development and the entrenchment of democracy.

Nelson Mandela, President of South Africa, address at the award ceremony, 1998

As a result of the very positive experience this architectural competition has produced, government recently agreed to adopt similar competitions as an alternative method for procuring designs for major government building projects.

Jeff Radebe, Minister of Public Works, address at the award ceremony, 1998

The chances are good that the winning entry will become a watershed in the history of South African architecture and that it will make a contribution to the development of a new style in architecture.

Charles Correa, Chief International Assessor, minutes of the competition steering committee

From Dream to Reality

the architects come on board
1998

The Five Finalists

There were eventually 185 formal entries for the first stage of the competition. Forty were from other countries. The jury chose five finalists – entry numbers 13, 49, 50, 69 and 120. Each of the finalists was given detailed inputs by the jurists so as to develop their ideas for the second and final stage of the competition.

ENTRY NUMBER 13

ENTRY NUMBER 49

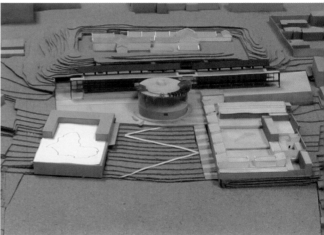

This is a design which, more than any other selected to enter the second stage, attempts to imbue the building with a sense of African-ness... The plan of the court chamber establishes a suitable balance between symbolic formality and approachability.... But the Jury are much concerned that, for all the welcome attempt to make the building symbolic of South Africa by taking as model essentially rural forms, the design may express no more than the pseudo-authenticity of the game lodge.

MICK PEARCE PARTNERSHIP

The clarity and simplicity of this scheme are impressive. The Jury welcome the way in which the building relates to the site and the care with which the prison has been incorporated... While the design is clearly capable of being a fine one, it could in a sense be anywhere and we believe it should respond more clearly to its role as a symbol of justice in South Africa.

JEFF STACEY, DESIGN PARTNERSHIPS

ENTRY NUMBER 50

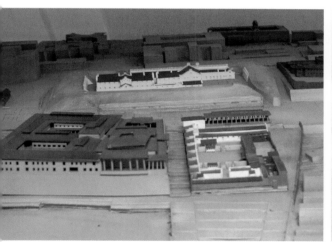

Generous and welcoming public spaces, both externally and inside the building, give this design distinction. The Jury is impressed by the proposal to use old bricks from the ATB to evoke memory of the past...The Jury is concerned that the court chamber is dreary and authoritarian... Developed in the wrong way, this design could topple into a parody of Colonial classicism.

JUSTIN SNELL

ENTRY NUMBER 69

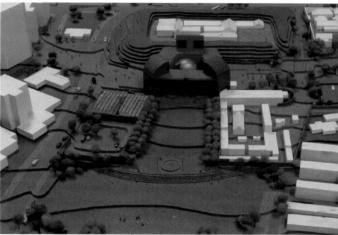

The Jury welcome the symbolism of the design, the three elements representing the judiciary, the public and the library holding hands and cradling the court chamber. However the clarity with which these forms is expressed leaves room for improvement. ...But planning is weak and unclear. Accessibility and entry need much more consideration...

HOLM JORDAAN PARTNERSHIP

ENTRY NUMBER 120

The Great African Steps combine with Constitution Square to form a fine
new series of public spaces at the junction of which the court chamber is
appropriately and symbolically located. The design respects the prison and
brings it into formal conversation with the new building. The robust vocabulary
of the design is welcome, though in development, it must be realised that the
building is to be a symbol of one of the most important aspects of the state.
The coloured image does not imply appropriate gravitas.

OMM DESIGN WORKSHOP AND URBAN SOLUTIONS

The five finalists' entries were posted up on panels in the City Council's Metro building. We'd limited the amount of space that people could use - I think it was three boards of a certain size. There was a great range of different concepts.

One entry was manifestly African. It picked up on the idea of three huge concrete huts that would have been dramatic on the hill. Another that the architects liked very much was the citadel, not dissimilar to the Alhambra in Granada; a third was a bold glass and steel structure in the modern idiom. I called it Danish. A fourth was based on the theme of family, it had a warm and friendly character. I called it the three bears.

The last one I called mish-mash because it wasn't clear what the building would be like. I had a feeling that a woman was involved because little buttons were used to show where the trees would be. It had a sense of anticipation, democracy. I loved it and so did Thenji.

Albie Sachs, *Constitutional Court judge*

Dear Minister, We, the jury of the architectural competition for the Constitutional Court building, have the honour of informing you that we have selected entry number 120 as the winning entry.

1. The Jury is of the opinion that the submission numbered 120 by the Competition Registrar is the winner of the competition. It has reached this conclusion because:

1.1 More than any other submission this one project has an image which is deemed to be appropriate to the aspirations of the competition brief.

1.2 It could be the pre-eminent building on the north slope of the site, not because of its monumental scale, but because it has the potential to express a new architecture which is rooted in the South African landscape, both physically and culturally.

1.3 The fragmented nature of the design disaggregates the built form to the scale of surrounding buildings. It is a conscious response to context and the need for construction methods which give opportunities for the exploitation of informal and alternative building procedures, technologies and material. This approach is more likely to succeed in revealing African trends than a self-conscious application of traditional stylistic elements or borrowing from European or historical building precedent.

Letter from the jury to Minister of Public Works Jeff Radebe, 13 March 1998

The Award Ceremony...

The winners were announced at a ceremony at the Old Fort on 8 April 1998. Everyone was delighted that when the identity of the finalists was finally revealed – four turned out to be South African and the other was from Zimbabwe.

The award ceremony was a joyous, fun occasion, and Mandela made the most of it. When he stood up to speak, he said 'I feel distinctly uncomfortable on this occasion, and in fact I'm wondering what I'm doing here at all.' I'd heard him on this kind of thing, so I'm grinning away, but my colleagues are getting quite alarmed. And he says 'Here I find myself sitting in the middle of a prison. I spent enough of my life there. As soon as the proceedings are over, I'm going to leave, just to make quite sure that nobody locks us up accidentally.'

Albie Sachs, Constitutional Court judge

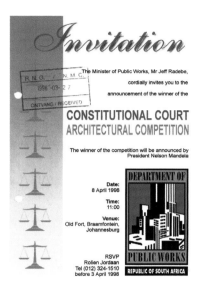

Invitation

R.N.G. / N.M.C.
1998-03-27
ONTVANG / RECEIVED

The Minister of Public Works, Mr Jeff Radebe, cordially invites you to the announcement of the winner of the

CONSTITUTIONAL COURT ARCHITECTURAL COMPETITION

The winner of the competition will be announced by President Nelson Mandela

Date: 8 April 1998
Time: 11:00
Venue: Old Fort, Braamfontein, Johannesburg

RSVP
Rolien Jordaan
Tel (012) 324-1510
before 3 April 1998

DEPARTMENT OF PUBLIC WORKS
REPUBLIC OF SOUTH AFRICA

The Court's physical foundations will rise from the horrific memories of torture and suffering which was perpetrated in the dark corners, cells and corridors of the Old Fort prison. Rising from the ashes of that ghastly era, this new institution will shine forth as a reminder for the future generation of our prevailing confidence and optimism that South Africa will never return to that abyss and indeed is a better place for all.

Nelson Mandela, extract from speech at the awards ceremony

CHIEF JUSTICE ARTHUR CHASKALSON AND NELSON MANDELA AT THE AWARDS CEREMONY Robert Botha, *Business Day*, Picturenet

And the Winner is...

At the end of his speech Mandela said 'And now I have the honour of presenting the winner of the competition. And the winner is …' And then he stops to take a drink from a glass of water. And he pauses, and says 'The winner is …' And he has another drink. Then he opens the envelope and announces 'OMM Design Workshop and Urban Solutions.'

Albie Sachs, Constitutional Court judge

DESIGNS ON THE CONSTITUTION: MINISTER OF PUBLIC WORKS JEFF RADEBE AND PRESIDENT NELSON MANDELA WITH JANINA MASOJADA, ERIK ORIS-HANSEN, ANDREW MAKIN AND PAUL WYGERS AT THE FUNCTION TO ANNOUNCE THE WINNERS OF THE CONSTITUTIONAL COURT DESIGN COMPETITION *The Mercury, 9 June 1998*

I get quite emotional looking back at some of the pictures when we won the competition. We were amazed. We were in the right place at the right time. We were young South Africans who embraced what was going on in our country. That gave us a huge advantage over the international submissions.

Janina Masojada, architect

I am heartened by the fact that although there have been entries from all over the world, a South African design has won.

Chief Justice Arthur Chaskalson, Citizen, 10 May 2001

It was nice to know that it was locals that won. They were nice kids.

Johann Kriegler, former Constitutional Court judge

The Winning Design

The winning team comprised three architects and an urban designer
– Janina Masojada, Andrew Makin, Erik Orts Hansen from OMM
Design Workshop in Durban and Paul Wygers from Urban Solutions
in Johannesburg. The team were young and passionate, and ready to
take on the challenges the new court building presented.

VIEW OF THE COURT CHAMBER FROM THE PUBLIC SQUARE

We decided 'If we're going to do this thing, we're going to do it to win.' And we loved it. We loved the process; we loved the engagement, the stimulation of it. It embodied all the ideas that we believed in. We worked really hard, we had the advantage that at the time we had no dependants, we could work 18 hours a day, smoke three packets of cigarettes. It was totally consuming.

Janina Masojada, architect

Two of the competition assessors - Charles Correa and Geoffrey Bawa - were our architectural 'heroes' at university. Their thinking and achievements nourished our understanding of the nature of architecture in a diverse, 'unresolved' society like ours (and theirs). And with Albie Sachs it was clear that this competition was as much about dignity and the essence of what it means to be alive and human, as it was about architecture. Having Thenjiwe Mtintso, then head of the Commission on Gender Equality, on the jury, gave us confidence - knowing the otherwise male jury was balanced by a powerful female voice.

Andrew Makin and Janina Masojada, Journal of the SA Institute of Architects, July/August 2004

More Than Just a Court

What set the winning design apart from the other entries was that it started from an urban design position. The design was an intervention that responded to the city around the court, making connections across and beyond the site.

Paul Wygers' urban design principles for the site also derived from observations of what makes cities work. The next question we had to ask ourselves was what makes cities democratic? And the answer here relates to choices. Democratic cities offer people choices - which, in turn, relates to freedom of movement, freedom of access, and appropriate, mixed land use that meets the needs of the people and offers them a range of amenities and opportunities, conveniently.

Andrew Makin, architect, Urban Green File Nov/Dec, 2003

Their design opened up the whole hill. The site wasn't the end of the journey. It was a place of thoroughfare and encounter - ongoing, mobile, fluid, moving - for people coming past. And connecting Hillbrow with Parktown with Braamfontein: the three totally different Johannesburgs.

Albie Sachs, Constitutional Court judge

NORTH EAST VIEW OF THE SITE TOWARDS HILLBROW, SOUTH WEST VIEW OF THE SITE TOWARDS BRAAMFONTEIN Athol Franz

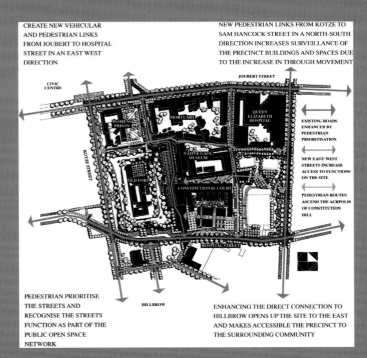

CREATE NEW VEHICULAR AND PEDESTRIAN LINKS FROM JOUBERT TO HOSPITAL STREET IN AN EAST WEST DIRECTION

NEW PEDESTRIAN LINKS FROM KOTZE TO SAM HANCOCK STREET IN A NORTH-SOUTH DIRECTION INCREASES SURVEILLANCE OF THE PRECINCT BUILDINGS AND SPACES DUE TO THE INCREASE IN THROUGH MOVEMENT

CIVIC CENTRE

JOUBERT STREET

WOMEN'S PRISON

MORTUARY

QUEEN ELIZABETH HOSPITAL

KOTZE STREET

NATIVE GAOL MUSEUM

OLD FORT

CONSTITUTIONAL COURT

HOSPITAL STREET

HILLBROW

EXISTING ROADS ENHANCED BY PEDESTRIAN PRIORITISATION

NEW EAST/ WEST STREETS INCREASE ACCESS TO FUNCTIONS ON THE SITE

PEDESTRIAN ROUTES ASCEND THE ACROPOLIS OF CONSTITUTION HILL.

PEDESTRIAN PRIORITISE THE STREETS AND RECOGNISE THE STREETS FUNCTION AS PART OF THE PUBLIC OPEN SPACE NETWORK

ENHANCING THE DIRECT CONNECTION TO HILLBROW OPENS UP THE SITE TO THE EAST AND MAKES ACCESSIBLE THE PRECINCT TO THE SURROUNDING COMMUNITY

Very early on I realised that there was only one place where you could put the Court - in juxtaposition with the Number Four. It was the only way you could ensure the thoroughfares across and through the Hill. Once we had decided on that and had established the journey between the two buildings, between the past and the present then all the other pieces fell into place.

Paul Wygers, architect

The Public Responds

The winning design attracted significant
attention from the public, the media and
the architectural profession.

This, the winning award, is architecture of a
high order; subtle symbolism, sensitive planning
for local conditions; an emphatic response to a
site of unique historic value; an assured, mature
aesthetic. It has in the assessors' words, 'the
potential to express a new architecture which
is rooted in the South African landscape, both
physically and culturally.

Alan Lipman article from The Sunday Independent, 3 May 1998

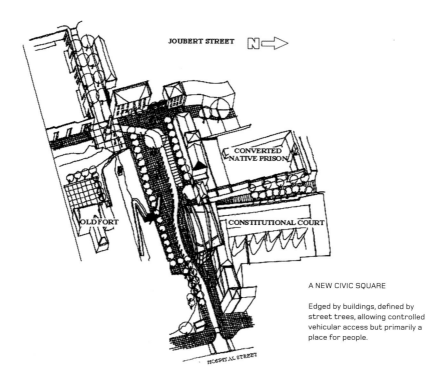

JOUBERT STREET   N⟹

CONVERTED
NATIVE PRISON

OLD FORT

CONSTITUTIONAL COURT

HOSPITAL STREET

A NEW CIVIC SQUARE

Edged by buildings, defined by
street trees, allowing controlled
vehicular access but primarily a
place for people.

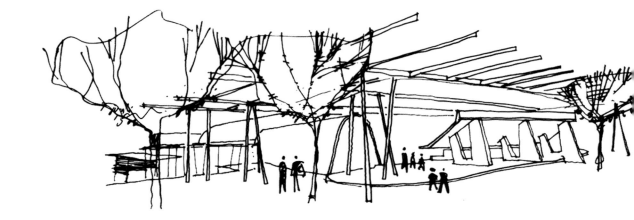

A building whose form contradicts the singular and inaccessible public buildings of the previous autocratic and dictatorial social structure.

SA Architect article entitled: 'A New Symbol for a New Democracy', subtitled 'The winning project OMM Design Workshop & Urban Solutions', pp 30-35

Grand dominant monuments are only needed to represent victories of war, exclusivity in the face of threat to an unpopular social system, economic or elite social power, or the unattainable – places of God or the gods. The Constitution, and therefore its houses and precinct, have nothing in common with any of these situations. The Constitution represents the opposite; an alternative means should be found to achieve symbolic importance for the building among the citizens of South Africa. We have chosen to seek the power of a pre eminent building without the monumentality.

'The Constitutional Court – A new symbol for democracy', 8 April 1998, Sachs archive

ARCHITECTURAL COMPETITION CONCEPTUAL DRAWINGS SHOWING THE BUILDING SITE INTEGRATED WITH PUBLIC SPACES

From Dream to Reality

The competition allowed the winning designers to dream up a court. But architects are all too familiar with the gap between initially conceiving a design and actually making the building happen. While the jury loved the ideas and spirit of the building, they had noted areas of the design that were open to question. Now was the time to thrash out the realities. The designers, the judges and two architects from the jury who had been asked to stay on as advisers – Willie Meyer and Herbert Prins – worked together as a team going forward.

They didn't adopt the attitude, 'What the hell! We won the competition and who has the cheek to tell us what to do.'

Herbert Prins, heritage consultant

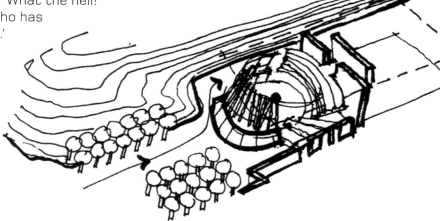

There was a lot of debate between ourselves and the judges. It was informal, it was engaging. We had exciting and stimulating interactions.

Janina Masojada, architect

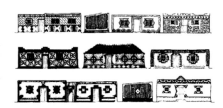
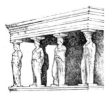

Debate and sometimes conflict arose on several key issues during the design process. The quest to develop a 'gravitas' for the court chamber, the position of the court chamber on the square or as a landmark element to the north, the architectural expression of the entrance foyer and the desire to discover new ways of dealing with conservative notions of heritage kept us discussing for hours. The correct choices seem to have been made but the debate continues to this day.

Paul Wygers, architect

Each section of the building was discussed with the relevant people - not only the judges but members of the library staff, the administrative staff, and so on. The architects encouraged that kind of process, and it was extraordinarily exciting to be part of it.

Kate O'Regan, Constitutional Court judge

We came up to Johannesburg and met with the building committee, made up of some of the judges and some members of the competition jury. They wanted us to assure them that in the course of design development the building would maintain its intentions and objectives. They said 'You won because of your conceptual ideas, and because of your document but we still don't know what the building looks like.' They wanted us to agree that as part of the design work, some of the jury would continue their involvement in the project.

Janina Masojada, architect

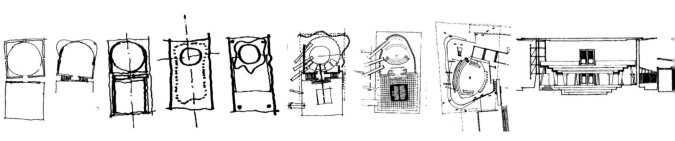

PRECEDENT IMAGES AND DESIGN EXPLORATIONS FOR THE COURT CHAMBER AND FOYER

Getting Going (or not?)

Great ideas were generated in the course of the discussions, but the project faced a budgetary crisis. R65 million had been allocated for the court building but this was not enough to cover the renovation of the prisons and the upgrading of the infrastructure such as the roads etc. The Department of Arts Culture Science and Technology (DACST) had come on board and were developing a plan for the entire precinct. There were now four proposed components – the Constitutional Court, the Constitutional Museum, the Nelson Mandela Library, and accommodation for the various commissions. But there was no money for any of this.

The site will accommodate all the commissions involved in the protection of human rights such as the Land Claims Court, the Human Rights Commission, the Gender Commission and a museum housing the process and history related the birth of the new constitution.

Chief Justice Arthur Chaskalson, City Press, 12 April, 1998

It was a very wobbly time: we had designed a building but we couldn't get to the front door; we had designed a parking lot but there was no road to get there. We had hired a team of people that we had to consider laying off.

Janina Masojada, architect

At the same time we were spending a lot of time thinking about the future of the Hill because the Court couldn't function as a completely solitary kind of stand-alone building surrounded by decrepitude. Gordon Metz, the chairperson of the Hill's Steering Committee from DACST, organised meetings to create an integrated vision for the overall development.

Albie Sachs, Constitutional Court judge

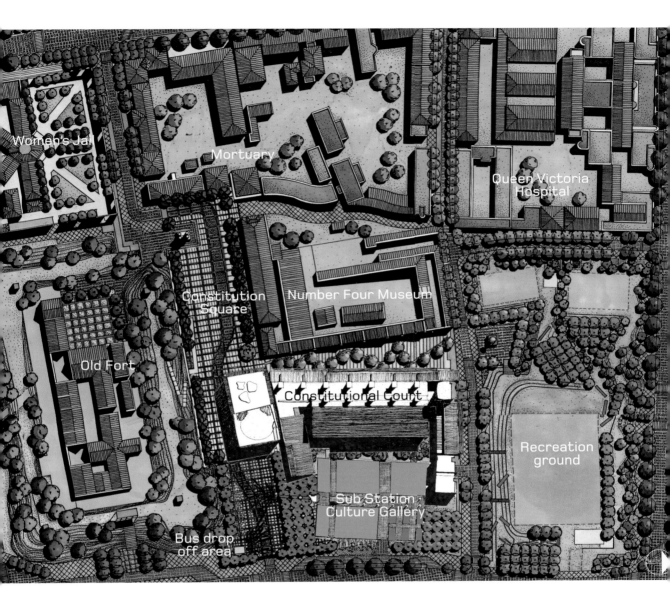

Women's Jail

Mortuary

Queen Victoria Hospital

Constitution Square

Number Four Museum

Old Fort

Constitutional Court

Recreation ground

Sub Station Culture Gallery

Bus drop off area

Different interested stakeholders and role-players came on board. But they were on board a rather stationary vehicle. Many of my colleagues were very dispirited. Johann Kriegler was totally gloomy. I was convinced that it would work, that this was a project that had enough backing to go through. But then the Department of Justice came back to us and said that they had no more money at all. The whole project was frozen.

Albie Sachs, Constitutional Court judge

Sinkholes and ripple ponds are two very important pillars of urban renewal strategies. Take the example of a very bad building. It's illegally occupied, the water's been switched off, there's no electricity or sewerage. Next door there's a very nice building, but the people next door don't want to live next to a building that is deteriorating so rapidly. They move out. Then that building becomes exactly the same as the one next to it. And so you start sucking in all the buildings around you and you create a large sinkhole situation. A ripple pond is exactly the opposite: it's when you throw a pebble into a pond and the ripples go out. The pebble in this case is Constitution Hill.

Neil Fraser, former executive director, CJP

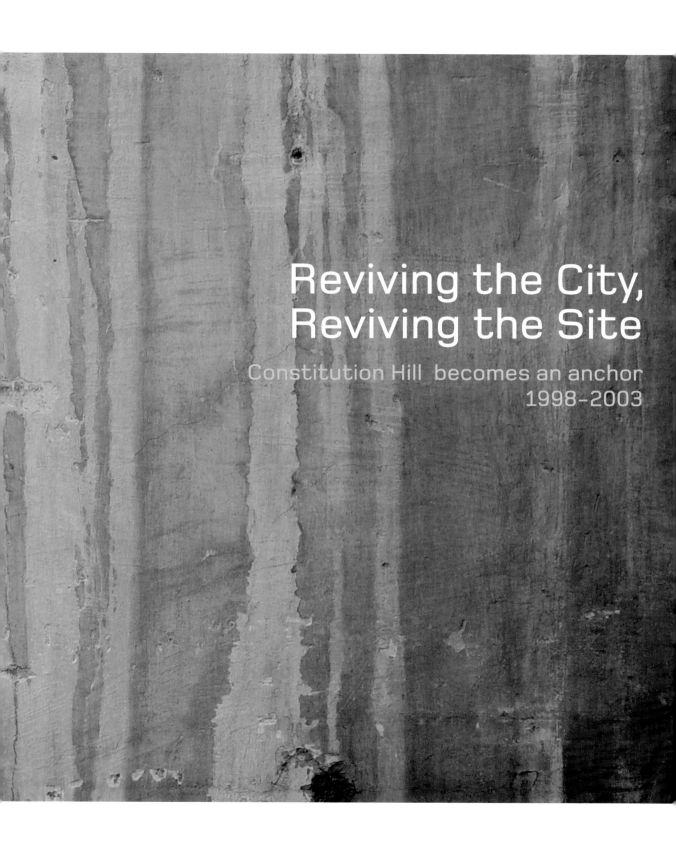

Reviving the City, Reviving the Site

Constitution Hill becomes an anchor
1998-2003

Moves in the Inner City

The process of building the court had come to a standstill. But the moves afoot in Johannesburg's inner city would ultimately save the development at Constitution Hill. Since the early 1990s, the inner city had been in rapid decline. Big business had moved out to the suburbs while there was an influx of people living in poorly maintained buildings. Now several interest groups wanted to reclaim the area for investment, growth and development. By 2000, with the election of the new city council, improvements in the inner city had become noticeable.

The state of the inner city during the early 1990s was portrayed in the media as an inexorable slide into a bottomless chasm - 'dying Johannesburg' - 'the soulless city' - 'a city in ruins'. Hotels closed, bank branches shut their doors and businesses lost confidence in the future of the city and moved north. Each closure was headlined in the press as 'another nail in the coffin' - no coffin was ever bound by so many nails! We brought together a group who still believed in the city - from community, local government and diehards from business. We worked initially at stopping the slide, a slow and difficult process as we jointly crafted a new vision for the city and a number of strategic interventions.

Neil Fraser, former executive director, CJP

DAILY LIFE AT THE NEW METRO MALL TAXI RANK ON THE OUTSKIRTS OF THE CITY CENTRE Brian Orlin

I joined the city in 1999 when the council was really beginning to focus on implementing the new vision to turn Joburg into an 'African World Class City'. We needed to create icons for the city similar to the Statue of Liberty in New York. We also wanted the right institutional and funding mechanisms to actually make these things happen.

Khetso Gordhan, former city manager of Johannesburg

With the emergence of Blue IQ, there was this emphasis on a proactive rather than reactive strategy in the city. They had a new dynamic approach, establishing points of growth and imagination and development rather than setting aside funding for routine budgetary needs.

Albie Sachs, Constitutional Court judge

It was around this time that Blue IQ was put in place by the Gauteng provincial government to kickstart projects. As general manager, I had to bridge grand ideals with implementation, I wanted to get things going.

Oren Fuchs, former general manager, Blue IQ

last picture **A VIEW OF THE MANDELA BRIDGE FROM BRAAMFONTEIN** Brian Orlin

Saving the Hill

The challenge with inner city projects is as much
reviving decaying infrastructure, as winning the
hearts and minds of the public. In Johannesburg
at that time, especially amongst the white public,
there was a tendency to negate everything that
was changing.

A big element of the battle was to convince people that government could
actually turn the inner city around through innovative means. We knew that
Constitution Hill would prove it could be done.

Oren Fuchs, former general manager Blue IQ

When Graeme Reid from the JDA said he's taking me to Constitution Hill, I
didn't know where it was. He said, 'It's just here.' I said, 'But I drive past that
place every day; I haven't seen anything there.' He said, 'That's exactly the
point. We want to put something there.' Inside it looked like a completely
hopeless place. But Graeme was passionate about it and he showed me the
proposed designs and how one could open it up and integrate it back into the
city. I quickly realised that Constitution Hill was part of the vision for a 'World
Class City'. I knew that it would become one of Joburg's new icons.

Khetso Gordhan, former city manager of Johannesburg

Khetso Gordhan convened a meeting with the Chief Justice, me and Jabu
Moleketi, the Gauteng finance minister and in charge of Blue IQ. He said,
'Here's this fantastic thing, but it's going nowhere because there's no
money. We as the city will put in R35 million.' And then Jabu said, 'Well, we as
the province will put in money as well.' Without people like Khetso, who just
made that decision without being bogged down by bureaucracy, and then
Jabu following suit with the backing of the province and Blue IQ, the project
wouldn't have been saved.

Graeme Reid, former CEO, JDA

The total public sector capital expenditure spent on the Court and infrastructure development amounted to approximately R469 million sourced from all three tiers of government:

- R70 million from the Departments of Public Works and Justice and Constitutional Development
- Land and R364million from Blue IQ (Gauteng Province)
- Land and R35 million from the City of Johannesburg

A further estimated R416 million in non-public sector funding is required to complete commercial, residential and Heritage, Education and Tourism components of the development.

Blue IQ (the province) and the Johannesburg Development Agency (the city) were crucial in getting Constitution Hill going. Both were set up by government and were accountable to government but functioned as commercial bodies, able to take quick decisions. They were able to facilitate private investment on the Hill so as to create a public/private partnership.

Blue IQ is a multi-billion rand initiative of the Gauteng Provincial Government with a specific mandate to invest in economic infrastructural development in ten mega projects in the areas of tourism, technology, transport and high value-added manufacturing, to create a truly 'smart' province. Blue IQ adopted Constitution Hill as one of its ten projects because of its tourism potential and the role it would play in reviving the inner city as well as having knock-on effects for the central business district.

The JDA was set up by the City of Johannesburg in 2001 to be the development agency for the City of Johannesburg. Its focus was inner city regeneration in the short term, and city-wide economic development in the long term. The Constitution Hill project targeted the creation of 6 000 short-term construction jobs and 500 sustainable long-term jobs and business opportunities. It set out to promote tourism to the inner city and to create a new source of rates revenue.

Getting Going

Even though the city and the province had agreed to come on board, several obstacles remained. The Department of Public Works still held the reins of the project. But the Johannesburg Development Agency (JDA), a new and unique institution, was in a better position to run an interdepartmental project of this nature.

We had quite heated negotiations with Public Works once the money was there, because they said, 'We're going to run the project.' The reality was that we would be able to build the court and deliver it in time for the opening on the tenth anniversary of democracy, which Public Works couldn't do. They were much slower because of government bureaucracy.

Graeme Reid, former CEO, JDA

It took us a good year of some very heavy negotiations with national government and with the city and to get all the parties involved to understand that we needed to take the project away from a single department because that was one of the reasons why it had not moved. We reached agreement at last and the building could begin.

Oren Fuchs, former general manager, Blue IQ

I was at the sod-turning ceremony at Constitution Hill
on October 21st 2001. It was attended by the Minister of
Justice and Constitutional Development, Penuell Maduna,
the Premier of Gauteng, Mbhazima Shilowa and the
President of the Constitutional Court, Justice Arthur
Chaskalson. It was far more than a ceremony to mark the
start of a new project. It actually was a celebration of
the end of an era of injustice, suffering and separation
and the start of an era of hope and of freedom. It
marked new beginnigs for the city.

Neil Fraser, citichat 42, 26 October 2001

CHIEF JUSTICE ARTHUR CHASKALSON, MINISTER PENUELL MADUNA AND PREMIER MBHAZIMA SHILOWA TURNING THE SOD Brian Orlin

The Builders

The winner of the R87.5 million tender to build the court and the infrastructure of the site was awarded to a joint venture between Rainbow Construction and WBHO. Chris Jiyane, the CEO of Rainbow Construction, was one of the few black architectural technicians who had managed to receive architectural training during the apartheid era.

I had followed developments surrounding the Constitutional Court before the project was awarded to my company. On the one hand, I had sad and painful memories of this place. On the other hand, there was this excitement of closing the ugly site with a view to opening it as the home of South Africa's new Constitutional Court. It was a very high profile project for our company. High profile, tricky finishes, tight deadlines and programme, and no room for mistakes.

Chris Jiyane, *CEO Rainbow Construction*

For me to be part of the construction of this place, which was the home to many of our political activists, is a great honour. It will be a symbol of hope for all the people of South Africa and I will do my best to ensure that it stands here forever.

Baldwin Matshidize, *trainee quantity surveyor on site,*
The Star, 24 June 2003

Our people fought hard during the struggle for a place like this. It is a privilege to be part of this, as many lives were lost so that this could become a reality. All the workers feel a sense of pride and it is going to be a magnificent building.

Simon Mhlongo, *builder of the Constitutional Court,*
The Star, 24 June 2003

THE TRAINING OF BLACK ARCHITECTS UNDER APARTHEID

In the 1980s, the Transvaal Institute of Architecture decided to do something about the fact that the facilities for black people to study architecture and allied disciplines were grossly inadequate. After lengthy negotiations, the apartheid government agreed that ten black people could be admitted to the Witwatersrand Technikon per year to study architecture. There was a further condition – the Institute had to undertake to build toilets for the black students on the roof of the technikon. The Institute selected and sponsored the ten black students.

When prospective contractors visited the Constitution Hill site, Mr Jiyane approached me and said that I might not remember him but he was one of the applicants whom I interviewed and accepted for the architectural technician's course. It is most gratifying to know that the efforts made all those years ago by the Institute have in at least one instance yielded such a wonderful result.

Herbert Prins, former President and member of the Transvaal Institute of Architecture, and President in Chief of the South African Institute of Architects.

BUILDERS ON SITE *top* Gisele Wulfsohn, *bottom* Brian Orlin

The Artists

The architects and the judges did not want to put up the Court building and then decorate it afterwards. They established an Artworks Committee to involve the arts community in the project from the beginning. The committee's first step was to invite artists to a briefing meeting on site. Then in February 2003, a formal call, known as the National Artwork Competitions, went out to all artists and crafters to submit artistic concepts for 31 identified artwork sites on the hill. These ranged from chimneys to wall tiles, steps, windows and other surfaces. R6 million was allocated for this purpose, much of it donated by foreign governments and foundations.

This is not a big 'White House' type of building. It is the elements that will make up the whole.

Janina Masojada, architect

from left to right **WILLEM BOSHOFF, STEVEN COHEN, JUSTICE ALBIE SACHS BRIEFING THE ARTISTS, MUSICIANS, BONGI NDHLOMO** Vanessa September

Like the Constitution, the Court belongs to and serves the whole nation. We want the eyes, hands and hearts of all our artists famous and unknown, to be involved. We do not want to acquire loose art and place it in the building but rather ensure that the art is integrated into the very fabric of the building. We want this to be a national project. We want to include people who don't even know they are artists. We want people who do beautiful doors, crafts and mosaics.

Albie Sachs, Constitutional Court judge

The Demolition of the Awaiting Trial Block

The design of the Court required the demolition of the Awaiting Trial Block (ATB) but the architects had planned ways for the prison to be commemorated. The old bricks were to be used to construct a wall of the court lobby and the court chamber as well as the Great African Steps. Four of the central stairwells were to be retained – two on Constitution Square, one inside the Court lobby and one just behind the court chamber. The Visitors' Centre was situated in what is now the foyer of the Court. It was chosen for reconstruction because symbolically it embodied what the larger structure signified – a cruel penal system. In 2006, it will be reconstructed in front of the Court, close to Hillbrow.

To salvage the bricks from the ATB meant that it had to be demolished carefully, almost brick by brick. There was no implosion or demolition by bulldozers. It was lovingly disassembled and the materials catalogued and stored. But despite the meticulous and laborious care, there was a complete lack of fanfare or ceremony. For me, who visited the site regularly during the demolition to monitor the process, the joy of seeing the project commence was tinged with sadness.

Herbert Prins, heritage consultant

Some still believe it should not have been demolished, and there is a great deal of validity in this argument. However, we decided that it was important to create an accessible public space at the centre of Constitution Hill that celebrated the right for people to gather, a right that had once been denied to most held there.

Janina Masojada, architect

THE DEMOLITION OF THE AWAITING TRIAL BLOCK *first image* Athol Franz Studio, *rest* Vanessa September and Brian Orlin

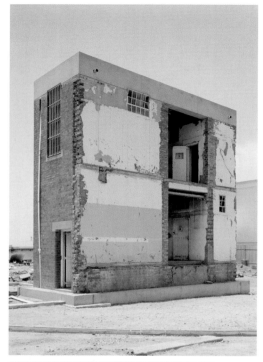

top THE REMAINING STAIRWELLS OF THE AWAITING TRIAL BLOCK ON CONSTITUTION SQUARE Andrew Meintjes
bottom THE PILLARS OF THE COURT LOBBY BEING BUILT IN FRONT OF ONE OF THE REMAINING STAIRWELLS OF THE AWAITING TRIAL BLOCK Vanessa September

Developing the Precinct and Opening the Site to the City

Once the building of the Court had begun, the rest of the project could be rolled out to give effect to the vision of developing the hill into a mixed-use campus. The precinct was designed to link up to surrounding streets to make the site accessible to the public and to become integral to the rebirth of the inner city.

The development was always much more than the Court building itself. When we first arrived on site, it felt like an island, walled off from the rest of the city. My immediate instinct was to develop it into a place with no physical controls - the opposite of a prison. The whole site had to become a thoroughfare - people had to be able to walk through it from Braamfontein to Hillbrow rather than going around it as well as feeling encouraged to hang out in a public space in that part of the city. In 2000, I participated in a process run by the Department of Arts Culture Science and Technology and the Department of Public Works to develop the master plan for the whole Hill.

Paul Wygers, urban designer

Around the core of the Court and the old prisons, the precinct would consist of series of interconnected public open spaces - Constitution Square, recreation grounds, the judges' gardens, the Great African Steps. Hospitality and retail outlets, a visitors' centre, a conference centre, archives and libraries, residential units and office space would be built on top of a large super basement to create a mixed-use precinct. These new buildings on the western side of the site are planned to open out onto Constitution Square. Also, a new set of buildings was planned in the courtyards of the Women's Jail.

Graeme Reid, former CEO, JDA

The public sector investment in Con Hill was seen as a signal of confidence in the future of the area. The ripple pond effect kicked in and a massive investment by the private sector started - investment in new buildings, refurbishing of existing and even in the upgrading of public space. This in turn sent a positive message to investors who had started flirting with the inner city redevelopment - the upturn was on its way!

Neil Fraser, former executive director, CJP

We had a project steamrolling ahead with building a
Court. And then we had all these heritage assets and we
were not 100 per cent sure what to do with them. The
huge question was, 'How do you make this site — a dark
hole in the centre of our city — available to the public
and legible to visitors?' And so the notion of Heritage,
Education and Tourism (HET) was born.

Graeme Reid, former CEO, JDA

Imagining the Hill

the founding of heritage,
education and tourism
2002

Appointing the Heritage, Education and Tourism Team

By the beginning of 2002, the building of the Constitutional Court, as well as the other parts of the precinct, was well under way. It was now time to start developing the heritage, education and tourism components of the site. In July 2002, the Johannesburg Development Agency (JDA) sent out a proposal to appoint a dedicated team to take forward the founding concepts of Heritage, Education and Tourism (HET). The tender to write the HET feasibility study and business plan for the site, was won by a consortium led by Ochre Communication, a film and communications company.

The notion of palimpsest that the winning team proposed and their ability to grasp the site and be bold and brave in terms of what it might be, made them stand out.

Graeme Reid, former CEO, JDA

We are storytellers at heart and from our first visit to the site, we felt the magnetic pull of the place and the amazing possibilities for revealing the histories of the buildings.

Lauren Segal, lead consultant, Ochre Media

We overcame the challenges of working in a three-dimensional space by drawing together an incredible multidisciplinary team of professionals - from architects to artists to historians. We also looked internationally to bring the best experience in museum planning and exhibition design. It is still one of the most memorable pitches I have ever been a part of.

Stan Joseph, CEO, Ochre Media

Constitution Hill is a palimpsest

A palimpsest is a surface on which the original writing has been erased to make way for new writing, but upon which traces of the old writing remain visible. The site is – and must remain – a place where the layers of history contained within it remain visible.

Ochre tender document, July 2002

GRAFFITI ON THE BACK OF THE ISOLATION CELL DOORS OF NUMBER FOUR Adam Broomberg and Oliver Chanarin

The Challenges Confronting HET

Heritage — stop the rot

In the beginning, it was a battle to integrate the heritage team into the development of the site. We came in after the architects and engineers had already been there for some years. They had established plans. The Court was already being built. Suddenly we arrived with a specific heritage agenda.

Dhianaraj Chetty, HET team, project manager

There wasn't always consensus amongst us. The site was falling apart and there was something incredibly moving, incredibly powerful about seeing nature reclaiming this place of pain. My initial instinct was to leave the buildings to fall down and let future generations watch them decay. Others in the team thought this approach was too radical.

Nina Cohen, HET team, architect

The challenge then became to restore the spaces and make them accessible to visitors without sanitising the prisons or destroying the ambience. We wanted to keep the sense of decay but we didn't want the buildings to collapse. We eventually came up with the term 'stop the rot'.

Nabeel Essa, HET team, architect

from left to right **THE ENTRANCE TO THE FORT, CELLS FOR SENTENCED PRISONERS IN THE FORT, STAIRWAY IN THE FORT ATRIUM** Andrew Meintjes

Education – how to become a human rights campus

We had to find strategies to ensure that Constitution Hill would be Johannesburg's Banyan Tree, where people could come together for leisure-time, to touch base with who they are and to explore issues of the present, such as reconciliation, human rights, citizenship and democracy.

Mark Gevisser, HET team, content

The education programme for learners and teachers needed to bring to life the values of the constitution and make connections between the past, present and future. The grand vision was that every South African learner should come to the site at least once in their school career.

Thembi Malao, HET team, education

Tourism – going from zero base

The Constitutional Court's decision to locate this site next to problematic Hillbrow made me think, 'Oh my goodness! What a daunting task it's going to be to try and get people to come here.' This place is also so visible, yet so invisible. It's right here in the middle of this city, people walk past it every day and yet it is not part of our consciousness.

Tshepo Nkosi, marketing director, JDA

There isn't a culture of visiting museums and galleries amongst the majority of South Africans. We realised we had to go deeper into understanding this.

Lucy Kaplan, HET team, tourism

DOORWAY TO THE COURTYARD OF THE FORT, COMMUNAL CELLS IN NUMBER FOUR, DOORWAY TO THE ISOLATION CELLS IN NUMBER FOUR Andrew Meintjes

The World Summit for Sustainable Development 2002

The Heritage, Tourism and Education team were mandated by the Johannesburg Development Agency and Blue IQ to embrace the challenges and learn about the site by opening exhibitions to the public during the World Summit for Sustainable Development. This plan was contrary to the conventional approach of starting a feasibility study and business plan by conducting desktop research and focus groups.

By chance, the HET team was appointed six weeks before the World Summit was due to open in Johannesburg. This was a big event for the city – the largest conference ever hosted here. This was an opportunity to showcase to the international community what we were trying to plan here, even if Constitution Hill was at that point a demolition site.

Tshepo Nkosi, marketing director, JDA

We jumped at the opportunity to give the public a chance to interact with the space. This seemed like a real litmus test of public reaction to the site, a useful starting point for the business plan.

Dhianaraj Chetty, HET team, project manager

Opening the site so soon after we arrived on the scene seemed like a risky strategy. There was very little time to create exhibitions and besides being a building site, the place was unknown as a tourist destination. But we realised that Constitution Hill's strength and uniqueness would be drawn from the ongoing interaction and participation of the public.

Mark Gevisser, HET team, content

VISITORS ARRIVING ON SITE DURING THE WORLD SUMMIT FOR SUSTAINABLE DEVELOPMENT Brian Orlin

The Memory Room

The Heritage, Education and Tourism team worked day and night to have the exhibitions ready and the site accessible for the first visitors. The Memory Room was the anchor project developed for the World Summit for Sustainable Development. Visitors were invited to listen to recordings of ex-prisoners talking, to record their own memories if they were ex-prisoners themselves or to share their responses to the development. This was a way of starting a database of public responses to the Hill. The first recordings were striking for the depth of emotions that the site evoked amongst visitors, young and old, black and white.

I wouldn't bring my family here because they would feel the hurt and the pain from the past.

High school learner, memory room transcript

My only wish is that our young people should get to know this place, they should listen to people's memories and know that they have a future to look after. They must keep this country as democratic as possible.

Vesta Smith, ex-prisoner, memory room transcript

This place makes me very sad. My stomach is shaking. People who were fighting for their rights were kept here unnecessarily. I think that they should develop this place so that everyone can learn about it.

Soweto resident, memory room transcript

We followed the rules of the former government in the same way as we follow the laws of today but we must show that it was wrong, that this is how it should be done. I am not shy about it and I would like to talk about these facts.

Pieter Swanepoel, ex-warder, memory room transcript

I think this place can bring more hatred. Maybe we can revolt again.

Hillbrow resident, memory room transcript

THE MEMORY ROOM Terry Kurgan

The Tunnel Exhibition

Three separate exhibitions were mounted during the World Summit for Sustainable Development. The exhibition in the tunnel beneath the ramparts paid tribute to the thousands of prisoners who had passed through the main entrance to the Jail, from horse thieves to Gandhi and Mandela as well as the hundreds of people who were caught at the wrong place at the wrong time.

The idea was to walk through a tunnel of ghosts – good ghosts and bad ghosts and everyone in between. We wanted people to have a sense of walking through history. You had to wind your way in.

Terry Kurgan, HET team, design

The Fort is not Robben Island. It's not a place where we can simply tell the heroic story of how activists were imprisoned because they fought for their freedom. The prisons here are altogether more complicated. Nelson Mandela and Gandhi were here. So too were violent criminals who deserved to be put away. But the vast majority of prisoners were the hundreds of thousands of ordinary people criminalised because of the colonial and apartheid race laws – pass offenders, curfew breakers, people arrested under the Immorality Act, beer-brewers.

Audrey Brown, HET team, content

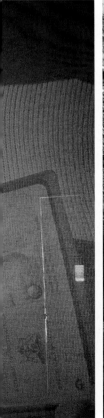

The History of the Future: Rampart Walk Exhibition

The ramparts were a perfect place to give visitors an orientation to the site, a physical and historical overview of the landscape in which the new Constitutional Court sits. The ramparts are one of the highest points on the Witwatersrand ridge, situated on a watershed. There is a sense from there of being on a cusp between two things; on one side you see the decaying Old Fort and on the other side you see the new Court.

The idea was to superimpose the historical and social issues embodied in the site and new constitution over the physical landscape of the site itself. We used a semi-transparent material onto which we printed text and images. Visitors then viewed the physical landscape through the image as a filter or lens.

Nina Cohen, HET team, architect

The exhibition evoked strong responses. This was the first time many school kids were exposed to this history. I remember one kid standing in front of the panel about a mixed-race couple who had been tried under the Immorality Act. Her own father was white and her mother black. She was shocked to learn that during apartheid this would have been illegal. Then one day we arrived to find the banner with the Communist Party image slashed. Someone had taken a knife to it. We realised that the past was far from dead and buried.

Tshepo Nkosi, marketing director, JDA

"What would I like to see at Constitution Hill?
I'd like to see a shopping centre, a crèche, a hair salon and a cinema."
Qoliswa Manasela, resident of 911 Burton Court.

The Three Women Exhibition

This exhibition was mounted in the atrium of the Women's Jail. An installation in silk, photographs and sound, it told the stories of three women who represented very different times in the Women's Jail's history and who were there for different reasons – Daisy de Melker, Nomathemba Constance Funani and Jeannie Noel – a murderer, a pass resister and a political activist, respectively.

For each of the women, we gathered together photographs and objects from different parts of their lives — we didn't only focus on the jail experience. I remember when Constance Funani walked in and the first thing she saw was the blown up image of the wedding photograph of her and husband, she was quite overcome with memory and emotion.

Terry Kurgan, HET team, design

I think it's a good thing to have had this opportunity to come here and be involved in the exhibition in the Women's Jail. We must build a place where our voices can be heard aloud so that when we are no longer around our children and their children will always understand what happened here, why this place is so important.

Constance Nomathemba Funani, ex-political prisoner

Nomathemba Funani died a few months after the exhibition was opened. It felt very significant that we had managed to record her story and pay tribute to her. It also made us realise the urgency of recording the life stories of prisoners, many of whom were old and dying.

Sharon Cort, HET team, research

The exhibition provoked strong debate about whether Daisy de Melker's story should have been exhibited. Should the story of a murderer be represented alongside far more noble people who had fought for their freedom and been unjustly imprisoned? It highlighted the importance of thinking about vastly different kinds of histories contained in the jails.

Audrey Brown, HET team, content

THE THREE WOMEN EXHIBITION Terry Kurgan, *top and bottom right* Gisele Wulfsohn, *bottom left* Brian Orlin

The Cleansing Ceremony

Just before the opening of the Three Women Exhibition, the Women's Jail was cleansed in a special ritual. Hundreds of people took part in the ceremony to prepare the Jail for a new development. Two new buildings designed by Kate Otten and Associates were to be built in the Jail's northern courtyard. The new buildings would house the Commission on Gender Equality as well as other commissions put in place by the new Constitution to strengthen constitutional democracy. The idea was that the old Jail building would be preserved as a museum amidst a thriving human rights precinct.

> The Women's Jail was once a place of abuse and humiliation for women. It's going to be transformed into a place where women and men come together to discuss gender equality. I couldn't be happier.

Xoliswa Falati, ex-prisoner, Sowetan Sunday World, 21 July 2002

> We do not want to fixate on the past; rather we want to release the souls and minds of women to fight against gender oppressions.

Joyce Piliso-Seroke, ex-political prisoner and chairperson of the Commission on Gender Equality, Sowetan Sunday World, 21 July 2002

PRAISE POET AND JOYCE SEROKE AT THE WOMEN'S JAIL CLEANSING CEREMONY Loren Barale

Reflections on the World Summit for Sustainable Development

The World Summit for Sustainable Development (WSSD) was a turning point. It marked the transformation of the site from a hidden place in the centre of the city to a public space where the pain of the past would be encountered and the new democracy celebrated. The experience provided the Heritage, Education and Tourism (HET) team with a sense of the key issue – the complexity of making stories of the prisons into exhibitions, the diversity of visitor responses to the site and the problems of running and maintaining a heritage precinct as large as Constitution Hill.

The WSSD alerted us to an essential contradiction of the site that is also the core of its energy: it needs to be both sacred space and living, vibrant space. Sacred, because of the ghosts who inhabit the prisons and the wisdom taking place inside the court; vibrant because it is the place where the constitution becomes a living, breathing document; a place where democracy is at work and at play. So one of our jobs going forward was to harness the energy created by the juxtaposition - the clash - of these two personalities; to understand that the one defines the other, just as a medieval cathedral opens out onto a bustling town square.

Mark Gevisser, *HET team, content*

Opening a building site as a tourist attraction proved to be tricky. The site had never been accessible to tourists and once the tourists were there, it was difficult for them to get around as there was a huge amount of building going on. But the exercise achieved what we had hoped for. It gave our team insights into the basic issues confronting HET. We were able to start formulating a vision and mission for heritage, education and tourism at Constitution Hill.

Dhianaraj Chetty, HET team, project manager

↘

HET Vision
Constitution Hill will become:
- a global beacon for human rights, democracy, and reconciliation
- a dynamo for empowerment and inner-city development
- a destination for local and international visitors
- a gateway from which to explore the rich heritage of Johannesburg
- a lekgotla where we talk to each other and the world
- a vantage point which gives us an understanding of our society in transition
- a refuge where our diversity is celebrated and our rights protected.

HET Mission
Our mission is to root the values of the Constitution and the issues they raise at Constitution Hill and thus render them physical – living, vibrant and interactive.

PANORAMIC VIEW OF THE SITE UNDER CONSTRUCTION Jo Ractliffe

Nelson Mandela, former President of South Africa, 2003

'We, the people of South Africa… adopt this constitution
as the supreme law of the Republic…'
Preamble to the Constitution of the Republic of South Africa, 1996

We The People

bringing people to the hill
and taking the hill to the people

CHIBUZOR NKEMDILIM AND BOY WITH HILLBROW IN THE BACKGROUND Adam Chanarin and Oliver Broomberg

The We The People Campaign

The We The People campaign was born out of the public engagement that began during the World Summit for Sustainable Development. The campaign was comprised of two sets of activities – Bringing the People to the Hill and Taking the Hill to the People. In Taking the Hill to the People, the team set out to communicate with people who lived in and around the site, such as Hillbrow and Braamfontein residents. Bringing the People to the Hill was launched to invite people who had historical relationships to the site, such as prisoners, warders, doctors, lawyers and chaplains, to tell their stories.

The WTP Campaign was designed to tap into the personal archives of our nation. The idea is that South Africans will become an integral part of the rebuilding of the site and the establishment of its exhibitions, rather than just the consumers of its products. They will have ownership of it.

Mark Gevisser, HET team, content

If we talk amongst ourselves, it's not enough. We need a period of discovery, a time when we get to understand fully what people think about certain ideas. We need to get a sense of buy-in from surrounding communities and from the country as a whole, to create a sense of participation in the building of this national asset.

Ralph Appelbaum, international museum consultant

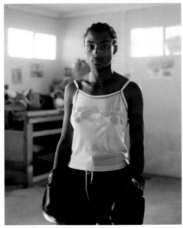

top REVEREND NOKUTHULA DHLADHLA – MAYFAIR, TESSA DAVIS – ELDORADO PARK, ANNALESI BHE – WESTERN CAPE, *middle* RICHTERSVELD
bottom GLYNN MORRIS WITH HIS CHILDREN – THE KAROO, DANI RAYMOND – WELKOM, GERT FOMROCH – RICHTERSVELD Adam Broomberg and Oliver Chanarin

MANDLENKOSI NOQHAYI – TRANSKEI Adam Broomberg and Oliver Chanarin

Taking the Hill to the People

Taking the Hill to the People began in Hillbrow, the community on the doorstep of the site. The judges' and Johannesburg Development Agency's vision had always been for Hillbrow to become part of the development and for the community to derive social and economic benefits from the Hill. Researchers took to the streets to conduct interviews with a wide range of people from sex workers to religious organisations. The team had specific objectives – to inform people of the plans for Constitution Hill, to learn more about the community and to establish a hierarchy of needs.

The Judges chose the site precisely because of its proximity to Hillbrow so it was important to work with this community. We also understood from rural ecotourism developments that the way to ensure the sustainability of a tourism project is to make sure that the host community owns it.

Lucy Kaplan, HET team, tourism

VIEW OF THE SITE FROM AN APARTMENT BLOCK IN HILLBROW Gisele Wulfsohn

Doing research in Hillbrow is complicated. On the one hand, there is a community of schools and churches and ordinary families trying to live their lives and raise their children. On the other hand, it is a transitory population and many people live in the area for five or so years before moving on. People have different relationships with the neighbourhood.

Ereshnee Naidoo, HET team, research

We spoke to the people who literally overlooked the precinct. Although they had fabulous views over the construction site across the road, they knew *nothing* about what was going on. In fact, they seem to have purposely blocked their views with their washing lines. It said something profound to us about how alienated these people are from their environment. And yet cities are about eye contact, about sharing space. It told us something about how daunting the task is of creating meaningful public space in the inner city.

Mark Gevisser, HET team, content

THE APARTMENT BLOCK IN HILLBROW FROM WHERE THE PHOTO WAS TAKEN Gisele Wulfsohn

Responses from the Hillbrow Community

People of Hillbrow should know that Hillbrow is not just a place of drugs, crime and prostitution. The history of this country started in Hillbrow - not in Rivonia or on the Island.
Hillbrow resident

VIEW OF HILLBROW FROM THE RAMPARTS Guto Bussab

We need a study space, newspapers, magazines and an information desk where people can find out about jobs and accommodation. The architectural marvels can come later on.
Hillbrow resident

Constitution Hill must be alive, not a sterile monument. People want to go to places where there's music playing, street theatre, dancing. It mustn't be stuffy, serious and worthy. I think sometimes the plans might be for some marvellous architectural construction, some great landmark, when all you actually need is a practical, useful facility.
Alistair Marshall, Hillbrow Library

I'd like to see a shopping centre, a crèche, a hair salon and a cinema.
Xoliswa Manasela, Hillbrow resident

Constitution Hill is contributing towards our approach of building more sustainable communities. If we have this development in the area, we can say, 'If I live around that, at least there is something positive here and a better picture'. People must know that Constitution Hill is their property. Then they will own it.
Ward Councillor Tyobeka

Constitution Hill should be a forum for debate and for participatory democracy, so that people don't only decide things for us but we as South Africans participate in the representative kind of democracy that we have here now.
Youth organisation leader

The We The People Road Trip

Understanding the needs of the host community was one aspect of Taking the Hill to the People. Heritage, Education and Tourism (HET) also wanted to understand more broadly how the constitution had impacted on people's lives during the first ten years of democracy. A team set off on a road trip to interview people, collect stories and capture photographic portraits of a diverse range of South Africans. The result of this was to be the We the People photographic exhibition which would be mounted for the opening of the Hill.

The team drove thousands of kilometres and covered all nine provinces of the country. They set out with the questions: Is it easier to love in the new South Africa? Is it easier to own a home? Is it easier to dream? Is it easier to be together? Is it easier to live?

Karima Effendi, HET team, road trip co-ordinator

The stories that stand out for me are those that we stumbled on. The story, for example, of an aged white Afrikaans-speaking male and a young black woman who steered a train to the border. After working together for years, they had developed a camaraderie that would not have been possible ten years ago.

President Kapa, soundman

OLIVER CHANARIN, MICKEY FONSECA, ADAM BROOMBERG AND PRESIDENT KAPA Self timer

Mr Mkhize's story sums up the optimism and the frustration that we encountered on the road. When we met him, he told us that he had only been photographed twice before in his life. The first time was for his pass book. The second was for his new identity book that allowed him to vote in the first democratic elections. Ten years later we took his picture. Mr Mkhize told us that he is still a migrant worker and lives in the same hostel. But ten years ago, the field in front of the hostel was a battleground between the IFP and the ANC. Today it's a football pitch. And he no longer shares his room with eight other men. Now he lives here with his wife for the first time in their married life.

Adam Broomberg and Oliver Chanarin, photographers

We visited communities and people who had been involved in Constitutional Court cases. When we drove into Richtersveld in the Northern Cape, the Court had just awarded the community its rights to claim the land. The impact of the constitutional process was being realised. History was unfolding before our eyes.

Mickey Fonseca, HET team, research

top **ADAM BROOMBERG and OLIVER CHANARIN** Mickey Fonseca *bottom* **MICKEY FONSECA** Adam Broomberg and Oliver Chanarin

Bringing the People to the Hill

While one team was on the road, another set about organising on-site workshops with ex-prisoners and warders. Ex-prisoners were invited back in groups according to the prison and the years in which they were held. Through the prisoners' re-enactment of their experiences in Number Four, the team was hoping to understand the layout of the prison, its rhythm, its culture and the changes that were implemented over time.

In the beginning, we relied on interacting with ex-political prisoners who were easy to find through our own networks and through veterans' organisations. But even well-known political activists like Juby Mayet gave me a tough time and said, 'Hey, come to that cop shop? Are you crazy?' I said, 'Look Jubs, we spent a long time here and if you don't come and tell the truth, somebody else will write what they like about this place.'

Nikiwe Deborah Matshoba, ex-political prisoner and HET team researcher

It wasn't an easy process to locate the ex-prisoners. There were no lists that we could refer to. We had piles of prison registers with names of those who had been incarcerated but no contact details. We didn't even know if the people in the registers were still alive.
Thapelo Joy Pelo, HET team, oral history

JOY PELO COLLECTING INFORMATION FROM EX-PRISONERS ON THE OPEN DAY Oscar G

My stepmother was the most difficult person to convince to come back. I had to think hard about upsetting delicately poised family relationships in order to persuade her. In the end, I was motivated by the fact that there were so many others like me who knew nothing about the role their grandmothers and mothers had played in ending apartheid. They had experienced the fallout but they didn't understand the story. I had to join the dots for myself. And I had to leave tracks for others to be able to do the same.

Audrey Brown, HET team, content

There was a lot of pain associated with coming back here. I remember one woman crying over the phone, 'I don't want to see that place.' I told her my story and how talking out at the Truth and Reconciliation Commission had helped me. This built trust because it encouraged her to believe that if I could do it, she could too.

Nikiwe Deborah Matshoba, ex-political prisoner and HET team, researcher

above ASSIENAH MNISI, AUDREY BROWN, JOHANA TIKI MOTHIMUNYE AND BELLA DLAMINI ATTENDING THEIR FIRST ON-SITE WORKSHOP
below JOYCE DIPALE BEING COMFORTED BY NIKIWE DEBORAH MATSHOBA Oscar G

Pan African Congress (PAC) Political Prisoners – 1960s

One of the first workshops held was with the political veterans of the Sharpeville era. This group launched the anti-pass campaign by leaving their passbooks at home and surrendering to the nearest police station for arrest. The State of Emergency was declared a week after and all known activists were detained. Most of the ex-prisoners were now old men but they were able to recall in minute detail the humiliating process of being admitted into the jail, of being stripped naked and forced to *tausa*.

I will never forget the eloquence of one of the men when he saw that their prison building had been demolished. 'This place,' said Victor Nkabinde, 'given that the roof is gone, it no longer has the same impact it had on me when I was kept here. There is a little bit of freedom now that I can see the sky. But the anger is not gone.'

Churchill Madikida, HET team, collections

left to right CORNELIUS MOTSUMI MPSHE (MANOTO), ISAAC HLATSHWAYO, THOMAS MNDANISO, JOHN MOKETSI MAHAPA, DAVID MASEKO, EDWARD SONNYBOY BHENGU, PAUL LUKHELE, EZEKIEL MAFORI MOTIMELE, PETER MOEKETSI, VICTOR SIPHO NKABINDE, WHITE SISINYI, ADDINGTON DLOVA, JOHN MOTHIBI GAANAKGOMO, JOHN FAKAZI MDAKANE

THE GROUP OF PAC EX-PRISONERS ON THE FORT PARADE GROUND WHERE, AFTER BEING REGISTERED AS PRISONERS, THEY ONCE MARCHED ON THEIR WAY TO THE AWAITING TRIAL BLOCK Oscar G

We climbed the remaining stairwells of where we were once held. We sang *Nkosi Sikelel' iAfrika* (God Bless Africa) and we remembered Sobukwe's words that to be in jail for one's beliefs was the highest sacrifice that man could make. We wanted our children and grandchildren to understand that.

Mr Gaanakgomo, ex-political prisoner, 1960

They told us how the whole prison would shake after they started singing the national anthem because every cell would join in and eventually the whole prison would be singing. It struck me how when one is incarcerated, you surrender control over your life. But just through singing you can terrify the authorities and bring the walls down. For me, that's the most powerful story I've ever heard.

Thapelo Joy Pelo, HET team, oral history

front row left to right EDWARD SONNYBOY BHENGU, ISAAC HLATSHWAYO, EZEKILE MAFORI MOTIMELE (WITH CAP IN HAND), DAVID MASEKO
middle row WHITE SISINYI, JOHN MOKETSI MAHAPA (HAND ON CHIN AND CROUCHING)
back row THOMAS MNDANISO (STANDING WITH HAND ON EAR), PETER MOEKETSI, CREW MEMBER

African National Congress (ANC) Political Prisoners – 1980s

left to right PREMA NAIDOO, SURESH NANABY, ALAN FINE, SAM KEKENE DESCRIBING THE EXPERIENCE OF REGISTRATION IN THE RECEPTION ROOM OF THE OLD FORT Oscar G

top SAM KIKINE AND SISA NJIKELANA IN THE NORTHERN COURTYARD OF THE WOMEN'S JAIL Oscar G
bottom SISA NJIKELANA REMEMBERING HIS EXPERIENCES OF BEING A PRISONER Oscar G

Black Women Political Prisoners – 1976

The women who were held in the Women's Jail in the period following the student uprising of 1976 came from all walks of life – journalists and teachers, community workers and academics. They spoke forcefully of being incarcerated in isolation cells that had since been demolished and of resisting the system.

I felt privileged to be part of this reunion. It was incredible to bear witness to the stories that unfolded as we walked around. But what has stayed with me the most, is the power of this group of women. One could sense the disruption their presence must have caused at the Jail.

Lauren Segal, HET team, project manager

MMAGAUTA A MOLEFE STANDING OUTSIDE THE ISOLATION CELL IN WHICH SHE WAS IMPRISONED AFTER THE SOWETO UPRISING IN 1976 Oscar G

It was weird walking through those huge wooden doors of Number Four Women's Prison of my own free will twenty-seven years after my detention in this place. Then it had been scary and unnerving and I hadn't known how long I'd be there, kept away from my eight children. This time I was elated. I could turn around and walk right out again without any qualms and no one would try and stop me. Number Four was changed. Our zinc cells were no longer there. Other parts had been spruced up. But for me, the big change was that it was no longer a place of fear, but a place of hope for the future.

Juby Mayet, ex-political prisoner

To remember those days and to remember all the experiences that we had together was very important for us. It was equally good to meet old friends, people that I shared accommodation with, my inmates.

Nikiwe Deborah Matshoba, ex-political prisoner and HET team, researcher

This day was profound for me. My stepmother and grandmother were both in the group. For the first time, I was able to understand the context of my life. I could fill the gaps in family stories and find the connection between myself, my family and the thousands of others who had been forced through these doors.

Audrey Brown, HET team, content

top - left to right VESTA SMITH, MMAGAUTA A MOLEFE, MALESHANE 'MALLY' MOKOENA MEETING UP AT THE FIRST WORKSHOP OF EX-POLITICAL PRISONERS FROM 1976 Oscar G
bottom - left to right JEANNIE NOEL, ZUBEIDA 'JUBY' MAYET, NIKIWE DEBORAH MATSHOBA, FATIMA MEER, CECILIE PALMER
RECOUNTING THEIR EXPERIENCES OF ENTERING THE WOMEN'S JAIL Oscar G

Black Women Political Prisoners – 1980s

SEPATI MORE REMEMBERING HER TIME AS A YOUNG STUDENT IN THE WOMEN'S JAIL IN THE 1980s Oscar G

White Women Political Prisoners – 1960s and 1980s

White women were held in a separate section of the jail. They were not allowed any contact with black prisoners except when black prisoners were brought to the doctor's rooms in the white section. Rica Hodgson, Esther Barsel and Barbara Hogan were amongst the first women to return to the white section of the jail to tell their stories. They remembered the harsh and cruel regime of the jail. They remembered the solidarity they felt with their fellow black prisoners despite the racial separation enforced by the prison system.

RICA HODGSON IN THE COURTYARD OF THE WHITE WOMEN'S SECTION Oscar G

The first time I came back to the jail was quite traumatic. My daughter Merle, who works at the Constitutional Court library, had brought me here. During the workshops, it didn't have the same effect on me. I felt glad that Number Four, as we called the jail, was finally going to be open to the public. But I was sorry that the white section was being painted and cleaned up. During the workshop process it was nice to meet the other African prisoners and exchange experiences with them.

Esther Barsel, ex-political prisoner

I don't have very pleasant memories of this place at all, except there was green grass and there were gardens.

Rica Hodgson, ex-political prisoner

Coming back here together today, reminds me of how Esther used to tell me about her experiences here. The memories of what Esther had gone through, the stories that she filled me with, were a kind of preparation for my own incarceration here. I have never said this to Esther before, but her talking about prison was absolutely invaluable for me. It was sort of like feeling that there were people around you who understood, because just knowing that you were following in a political tradition was a remarkable thing.

Barbara Hogan, ex-political prisoner

These women were very inspiring. They were conscious agents who chose to fight apartheid at a time when so many others preferred to accept the rewards the system offered them and to ignore the suffering of millions of people. They chose jail, exile and ostracism, rather than accept apartheid.

Audrey Brown, HET team, content

RICA HODGSON, BARBARA HOGAN, ESTHER BARSEL DURING THEIR FIRST ON-SITE WORKSHOP Oscar G

Nelson Mandela visits Constitution Hill

Nelson Mandela was imprisoned at Number Four three times – first during the Treason Trial in 1956 and then again in 1958 and 1962. During his last stay, Mandela had the dubious honour of being the only black prisoner to be held in the Old Fort, the prison for white males. The team were very keen to bring back to the site the most famous prisoner in the world.

Interviewing Mandela about his time at the Fort was a difficult but illuminating experience. Whenever I asked him to recollect any detail, he responded: 'I'm a very old man. I'm a hundred years old. Don't ask me to remember…' He was willing to talk about building the future by remembering the past. But it was clear that he no longer wished to dwell on his *own* past. He was using what precious little time and energy he had left to deal with urgent matters of the present, like reconciliation and the fight against AIDS.

Mark Gevisser, HET team, content

NELSON MANDELA IN THE ENTRANCE OF THE HOSPITAL CELL IN THE OLD FORT DURING HIS VISIT TO CONSTITUTION HILL IN DECEMBER 2003 Oscar G

Watching Madiba wave and smile to the scores of workers who were completing the building made me cry. There was a light in his face and in theirs. Here were young men fashioning the bricks of the old prison into the new Constitutional Court, waving and smiling at an old man who'd been imprisoned here so that they would be free. I was laughing through my tears.

Audrey Brown, HET team, content

You must know your past and the cruelty that was committed to your people. But don't keep this too much in mind because we are here to build a new South Africa. That is what you must commit yourselves to. You must remember what has happened in the past so that, in future, you can avoid it.

Nelson Mandela, former President of South Africa

left to right GEORGE BIZOS, NELSON MANDELA, AHMED KATHRADA AND CHIEF JUSTICE ARTHUR CHASKALSON
INSIDE THE HOSPITAL CELL WHERE MANDELA WAS IMPRISONED IN 1962 Oscar G

EX-PRISONER RETURNING FOR THE FIRST TIME TO THE LAUNDRY ROOM WHERE SHE ONCE WORKED IN THE WOMEN'S JAIL DURING THE OPEN DAY Oscar G

The Open Day

The We The People team was gaining many important insights through the workshops with the political prisoners. But it was very important for the team to reach the ordinary people who had found themselves on the wrong side of apartheid law and ended up in Number Four. The team organised an open day on site. A call went out to the public through newspapers and community radio stations to invite ex-prisoners to return to Number Four on 22 November 2003.

The distress of the women who came back that day was very disturbing and cast a strange new light on the jail. It forced us to reconsider our representation of the spaces. It became clear that the jail was not just a space where strong, politically motivated women forged unbreakable bonds with each other and unshakeable political convictions. These ordinary women were traumatised and harassed, beaten and, in some cases, broken by the experience.

Audrey Brown, HET team, content

There were differences between the way the men and the women responded during the open day. The men didn't want to deal with the pain but a lot of the women cried and some were seriously traumatised, just telling their stories for the first time.

Thapelo Joy Pelo, HET team, oral history

The people who came were indeed ordinary folk who we would never have reached through political channels. We took their details and they put us in touch with others. And so we started to develop a network of ordinary prisoners bit by bit.

Thapelo Joy Pelo, HET team, oral history

top **EX-PRISONERS AND VISITORS ARRIVING AND REGISTERING AT OPEN DAY** Oscar G
middle **EX-PRISONERS AND VISITORS WATCHING AN ORIENTATION VIDEO ON CONSTITUTION HILL** Oscar G
bottom **YVONNE NTONTO MHLAULI SHOWING HOW WOMEN PRISONERS WERE FORCED TO SCRUB THE HARD FLOORS WITH THEIR BARE HANDS AND ON THEIR KNEES** Oscar G

Ordinary Prisoners in Number Four

After the open day, groups of ex-prisoners were invited back to site for more formal workshops. Some were violent criminals - murderers, rapists and robbers. Others were held for apartheid offences. All had important stories to tell.

I am still haunted by the eyes of a man who introduced himself to me as Xikwembu xa Yina which means God Almighty in Shangaan. I asked him why he was called that. He bragged that in Number Four he could decide if people like me would live or die. I also often shared a cigarette and exchanged jokes with Bra Jack, who told me in vivid detail how he boxed a man to death for a tin of polish.

Steve Kwena Mokwena, HET team, curator

You got a sense from the political prisoners that they were used to telling these prison stories, they came here as part of their duty because they understood the political importance of these stories being recorded. The ordinary criminals were far more tentative to start off with. They did not have a sense of the process. But they were far more emotional.

Steve Kwena Mokwena, HET team, curator

EX-PRISONERS RE-ENACTING THE REGISTRATION PROCESS, SHOWING WHERE PRISONERS' THUMBPRINTS WERE TAKEN AND HOW PRISONERS USED TO GET BEATEN IF THEY DISOBEYED PROCEDURES Oscar G

I found it extremely difficult to watch these men adopt the body language of inmates. They were flung back to a time when they had no autonomy and no dignity. And in a way, so were we as we watched them crouch and squat with their heads tucked in, eyes downcast and hands behind their backs in the body language of a prisoner.

Audrey Brown, *HET team, content*

from left to right SIPHO SIBIYA, JABULANI MADONSELA, JACOB WESI, JACK MABASO LINING UP IN THE DOORS OF THE ISOLATION CELLS IN NUMBER FOUR

Ordinary Women Prisoners

top left DAPHNE NENE IN THE COURTYARD OF THE WHITE WOMEN'S SECTION Oscar G
top right PATRICIA ALARM AND JOHANA 'TIKI' MOTHIMUNYE EXPLAINING THE LAYOUT OF THE COMMUNAL CELLS Oscar G
bottom left PATRICIA ALARM EXPLAINING HOW PRISONERS WERE NOT ALLOWED TO WALK THROUGH THE MIDDLE OF THE WOMEN'S JAIL ATRIUM Oscar G
bottom right NOLUNDI NTAMO, PALESA MUSA, YVONNE NTONTO MHLAULI IN THE LAUNDRY ROOM Oscar G

ASSIENAH MNISI, JOHANA 'TIKI' MOTHIMUNYE, BELLA DLAMINI, PATRICIA ALARM STANDING
ON THE STAIRS LEADING UP TO THE WHITE WARDERS' LIVING QUARTERS Oscar G

The Warders

...t grandeur...
...e of **stark** naked women, their arms o...
...e first floor. I had a...
being searched by the vagaash (warder). I sa...
...n the ball in progress, but wa...
embarrassment in their **eyes** and look...

Fatima Meer

€

fleeting

EX–WARDER, MARTIN 'PANYAZA' SHABANGU, IN FRONT OF THE GUARD HOUSE IN NUMBER FOUR Oscar G

Prisoners invariably have a fragmented sense of the spaces in which they were once incarcerated. They were only allowed into certain parts of the jail and they were often forced to walk chuffkop - with their heads bowed and their eyes downcast. The warders, in contrast, had a more complete picture of the jail and their experiences were an essential part of compiling the oral history.

The workshops with the warders had their own emotional tenor. Poignantly, a black male warder was moved to tears when he entered through a prison door that he was not allowed to use when the jail was still in operation.

Steve Kwena Mokwena, *HET team, curator*

We had to run separate workshops for black and white warders. The discrimination amongst the warders lay too close to the surface and many of them still work in the prison system today.

Churchill Madikida, *HET team, collections*

The warders were the most difficult groups to work with because we had to move ourselves beyond judgement of their self-serving justifications. We had to try and understand and accept that these people had been part of a larger system and that their stories were also valid. Some were even prompted by the workshops to accept responsibility for their actions. I overheard this one warder tell her daughter that it was an honour for her to help us understand the jail.

Audrey Brown, *HET team, content*

top THERESA SWANEPOEL AN EX-WARDRESS AT THE WOMEN'S JAIL IN FRONT OF AN IMAGE OF BABARBA HOGAN ON THE HOARDING ON CONSTITUTION SQUARE *bottom* EX-WARDRESSES AT THE WOMEN'S JAIL, LINDA XAMESE, MATRON LYDIA NOSILELA AND NOMBULELO BATANA IN FRONT OF THE HOARDING ON CONSTITUTION SQUARE Oscar G

An Emotional Journey

During the workshops, memories that had been buried for years rose to the surface. For some, the workshops brought back the pain and suffering that the prisoners had endured and opened fresh wounds. For others, the collective telling and retelling of the prison experiences, started a process of healing and brought a sense of closure to their experiences.

There was a time during the workshops when I used to have nightmares. Sometimes I woke up at night and I started thinking about what we had been through. I mean it was a long time that one spent in here. But I was strengthened by the fact that in the mid-seventies, the prison was a story about anger, bitterness and the language was that of war. Now it's different. Yes, it is a fight, but we are now fighting to preserve our heritage.

Nikiwe Deborah Matshoba, ex-political prisoner and HET team, researcher

There was so much to discover about the spaces in the jail. But finding out how many people had been held there made me realise how important this place was to the memory of black people. It was a fearful privilege to walk with them, to hear them scream with anguish and to finally listen to their memories. To stand in the doorway of a cell and coax a wailing woman to walk across the floor, quietly reminding her that she's free now, is a fearful privilege.

Audrey Brown, HET team, content

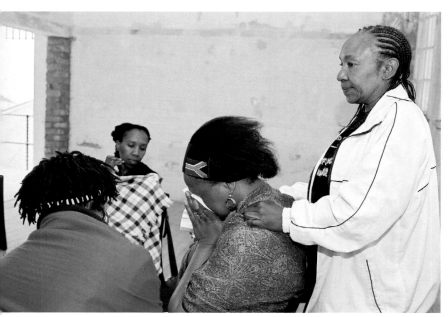

left **AUDREY BROWN, BABY TYAWA, LILIAN KEAGILE, NIKIWE DEBORAH MATSHOBA** Oscar G   *middle* **AUDREY BR** VN AND NOLUNDI NTAMO Oscar G

Before I participated in the workshops, I could never walk past this place. I live in Hillbrow but I could never walk down Kotze Street. After telling my story with the other ex-prisoners, I started to come and hang out here. Now I am part of the ex-prisoners forum that will run programmes on the site. I feel very good to see my story on the exhibition.

Yvonne Ntonto Mhlauli, ex-prisoner

right **AUDREY BROWN AND PALESA MUSA** Oscar G

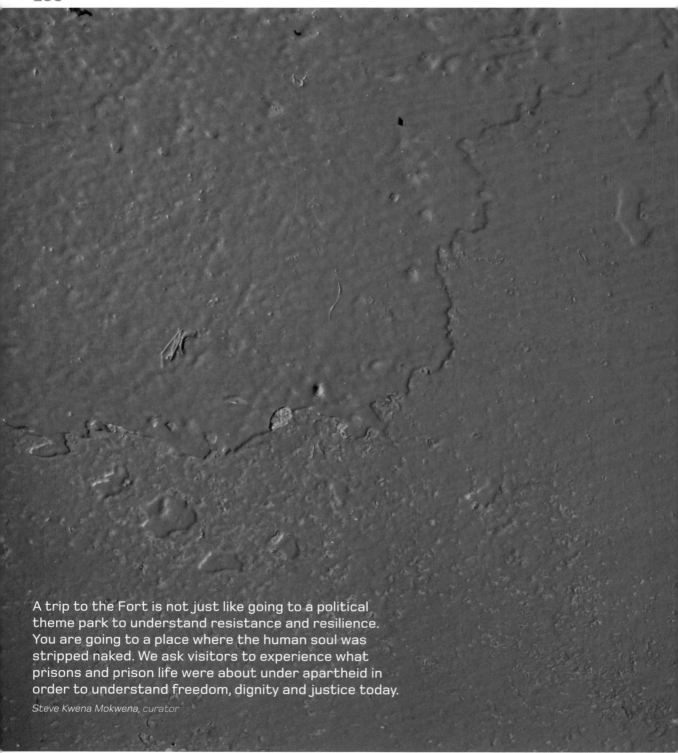

A trip to the Fort is not just like going to a political theme park to understand resistance and resilience. You are going to a place where the human soul was stripped naked. We ask visitors to experience what prisons and prison life were about under apartheid in order to understand freedom, dignity and justice today.

Steve Kwena Mokwena, curator

Responding to the Voices

the making of exhibitions and the visitor experience
2003-2004

Eight Months To Go

It was July 2003. The official opening of the Constitutional Court and the Hill was scheduled for Human Rights Day, 21 March 2004, just eight months away. There were multiple teams on site, each with their own set of challenges. The builders of the Court had to have it ready for the judges to move in during February 2004 and they were running behind schedule. The mortuary had to be relocated so that the building of the basement for parking could be started. And the Heritage, Education and Tourism (HET) team had to ensure that the museum was up and running in time for the opening of Constitution Hill.

Our task was to figure out a way to implement the ideas in the business plan and to develop a visitors' centre, create the initial exhibitions, establish a website, write brochures, develop educational material and train tour guides and staff to run the facility. The plan for this became known as STIP – short-term implementation plan.

Stan Joseph, CEO, Ochre Media

In August 2003, there was still no money to put STIP into action. Luckily, 2004 was the tenth anniversary of democracy in South Africa and the Ford, Mott and Kellogg Foundations saw the Constitution Hill development as a perfect opportunity to celebrate our young democracy. Their enthusiasm for the project and financial commitment kick-started STIP.

Graeme Reid, former CEO, JDA

When the money came through from the donors, we found ourselves with just six months to go until the doors of Constitution Hill would open. Our international consultants said we could never create a museum in that time. But we were naïve and excited. For months, we had been listening to ex-prisoners, warders and Hillbrow residents. We had engaged in endless discussions with the judges, experts, fellow curators and heritage advisers. Now the time had come to turn all these dialogues into something real and tangible for visitors.

Lauren Segal, HET curatorial team, project manager

Creating the Visitor Experience

The HET team had two immediate priorities. The first was to decide which facilities would be in place for the opening. The second was to figure out how to turn the wealth of oral testimonies, photographs and footage into exhibitions and installations which would constitute the first layer of interpretation for the site.

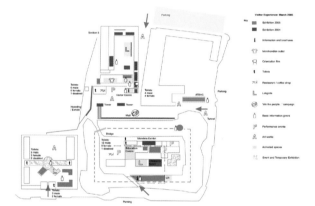

> We didn't want a museum with four walls. We wanted different spaces that told different stories so as to give the visitor a collective memory of what the site was and what it is going to be.
>
> *Tshepo Nkosi, marketing director, JDA*

The exercise felt very charged. Since 1994, debates on heritage and history, truth and reconciliation, memory and forgetting had featured prominently in South Africa. They were at the heart of what we were grappling with.

Mark Gevisser, HET curatorial team, content

At this point, we worked closely with Ralph Appelbaum, who designed the Holocaust Museum in Washington DC and Gail Lord from Lord Cultural Resources who had planned many museums. With the time constraints and the enormous importance of the project, their expertise was extremely valuable. They helped us trust in our instinct of minimum intervention, maximum impact.

Lauren Segal, HET curatorial team, project manager

Starting in Number Four

Limited funding and time constraints meant that choices had to be made about which physical spaces to interpret first. The curatorial team has always understood that the exhibitions would develop in an incremental and phased way. But now we had to ask ourselves where do think we should start? The site has three prisons – the Old Fort for white male prisoners; Number Four for black male prisoners, and the Women's Jail for both black and white women.

Number Four seemed like a logical and ideal starting point for the first exhibition. Firstly, Number Four occupies a central place in the history of black life in Johannesburg and has an almost mythical status. Secondly, the fact that the new Constitutional Court is built alongside and parallel to Number Four presented an ideal starting point to tell the story of South Africa's journey from a past that denied human dignity to a present founded on the cardinal principles of freedom, equality and dignity.

Steve Kwena Mokwena, HET curatorial team, curator

THE GREAT AFRICAN STEPS Andrew Meintjes

Heritage Versus Exhibition

Sections 4 and 5 had been abandoned for over twenty years
and were in a state of extreme disrepair. It was as if nature had
reclaimed a space where men had done evil, and the exhibition
team wished to preserve this sense. None the less, some of
the cells needed to be opened up, to allow for stories to be told
that would enhance the experience for visitors.

> There was suddenly a brilliant idea that a certain space should have some kind
> of an exhibition in it. Which in itself isn't a bad idea necessarily but then in order
> for it to work, there have to be electrical supplies, audio-visual material, air-
> conditioning, all these sort of things. You could argue that that's not so serious
> because it can be taken away, but in my opinion the things that go with an
> exhibition can totally damage, forever, the quality of the heritage.
>
> *Herbert Prins, heritage consultant*

ORIENTATION VIDEO AT THE ENTRANCE TO THE EXHIBITION Guto Bussab

The exhibition team were very clear that an important part of the power of Number Four was this sense of ruin. We did not want to make any interventions that would destroy the historical fabric of the site. Tensions none the less emerged between heritage concerns and those of the exhibition team.

Nabeel Essa, HET curatorial team, architect

For us, heritage is not just the building or the site. The recuperation of history and experience is as important as the preservation of bricks and mortar. This is particularly urgent in spaces where there was so much injustice and pain and where the voices of oppressed people were silenced. Our task was to provide a platform for those who had been silenced so that these spaces spoke a broader heritage than the buildings alone.

Clive van den Berg, HET curatorial team, designer

As the plans developed, the team found the need to use additional cells as exhibition spaces. This expansion into what was a holy heritage site created a concern that the original structure was being eaten into by the exhibitions.

David Cort, HET project manager

Curatorial Principles

With regard to **space**, exhibitions will:

- recognise that the site itself is the first exhibition
- be phased, incremental, evolutionary and responsive to visitor inputs
- be installed in multifunctional spaces
- emphasise the unique urban geography of the site, fostering a strong sense of the urban landscape as shared public history
- help establish inner-city Johannesburg as a desirable tourism destination and build a tourism economy in the inner city, and facilitate inner-city regeneration.

With regard to **content**, exhibitions will:

- bring alive the values of the Constitution of South Africa
- activate an interest in human rights and democratic citizenship
- interpret the past
- interpret contemporary society
- emphasise the relationship between the past, the present and the future.

With regard to **form**, exhibitions will:

- communicate through the personal register
- use multiple voices to tell the same story, acknowledging contemporary approaches to history, memory and heritage
- be multilingual
- be interactive, participative, responsive, accessible, experimental, and integrated
- cater to multiple audiences and several generations at the same time
- encourage popular participation and facilitate public ownership
- use innovative strategies to promote the growth and development of new audiences for museums and heritage sites.

Designing the Exhibitions

Once the spaces to be used were agreed on and the curatorial principles established, the design work could begin. Design had its own challenges - what languages were to be used so as best to convey the stories? How should different audiences be accommodated? Should the actual cells be recreated?

We did not want to reiterate or re-inscribe materials commonly used to memmorailise the past, like stone and bronze. These materials perpetuate the notion that the values of a time are permanent and irrevocable because the monuments would literally last forever. I felt very strongly, post-democracy, that we shouldn't rush into particular languages too quickly, that we should have a time to think about how we wanted to materialise the democracy, how we wanted to memorialise pain. I was much more interested in the absent, the fugitive, the non-material.

Clive van den Berg, HET curatorial team, designer

CELL   GEOGRAPHY

ABLUTIONS

Our own sense of what is an appropriate language changed as well. Fluidity was an essential part of the process. An ex-prisoner would arrive on site and give us a new piece of information which changed our notion of what a particular space meant and how that space could speak.

Clive van den Berg, HET curatorial team, designer

SLEEPING MAT

BLANKET

We had to wrestle with the prisoners about what really needed to happen with the site. They mostly wanted it to look like it did when they were imprisoned. We weren't convinced about this. I think that we wanted to memorialise the space, they wanted us to memorise it.

Audrey Brown, HET curatorial team, content

PERSONAL EFFECTS

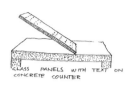

GLASS PANELS WITH TEXT ON
CONCRETE COUNTER

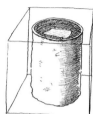

FOOD DRUMS WITH PIECES OF
PAPER STATING 'RACE' OF FOOD
GLASS VITRINES

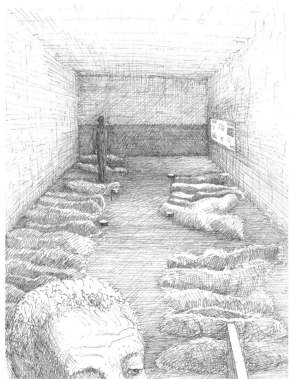

CONCEPT DRAWINGS OF THE EXHIBITION SPACES Clive van den Berg

Making the Exhibitions

The designers could not rely on a ready-made collection of objects and documents to create the installations. The exhibition demanded an entirely different approach. The ex-prisoners who participated in the workshop process were invited to become part of a team to realise the exhibition design. What could have been a problem turned into one of the most exciting aspects of the exhibition.

I recruited some of the ex-prisoners to work with us. They made a few samples of the blanket sculptures they made and the games they played in prison and I loved what I saw. I gathered the other curators and we decided that these things should be part of the exhibition. We tried to intervene with the ex-prisoners as little as possible. We tried to let the objects that they created tell their own stories.

Churchill Madikida, HET curatorial team, collections

There was so little time, and such a huge amount of work to produce and install. No project since this has given me the same intensity of work, except my own artwork. This is the only other situation I have encountered where you are creating and learning and rushing all at once. It produces a special kind of energy amongst those involved and it was an amazing experience.

Sean Slemon, exhibition manager

   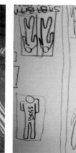

first picture ISAAC LUPHINDO AND VUSI TSHABALALA, BLANKET AND SOAP SCULPTURES IN THE MAKING Sean Slemon

Vusi Tshabalala was appointed as a permanent member of staff at Constitution Hill. Eighteen months after the exhibition opened, he was murdered for unknown reasons on the same corner where he was arrested and brought to Number Four in the mid-1970s.

I joined Number Four last year as a sculptor and engraver. I wasn't an artist. I learnt these things here in Number Four. When Church found me, I was working at part-time jobs. At first, I didn't like to work here. I was feeling very bad because I kept imagining the things that happened to me here. But as the days went on, I started to forget. Churchill told me, 'You are no more in prison. You mustn't think too much of this place. Take it as it comes, you are working here now.'

Vusi Tshabalala, ex-prisoner and blanket sculptor, 2005

The Walk-through

Prison dictates how a person moves, what they wear, what and how they eat, how they wash, where and how they sleep, what physical pain they are subjected to, and so on. Number Four was particularly brutal and the exhibition sought to give the visitor a sense of what the bodies of black men experienced in the space.

Steve Kwena Mokwena, HET curatorial team, curator

What we're doing at Constitution Hill is trying to disturb the preconceptions, the clichés, the comfort zones of historical perception.

Clive van den Berg, HET curatorial team, designer

Many of the stories of brutalisation and dehumanisation that characterised the Number Four experience continue to be commonplace in prisons today. Although the racial separation of prisoners may no longer be an issue, many prisons are still dealing with extreme forms of violence. It is important not to give the impression that all is well in the new South Africa.

Steve Kwena Mokwena, HET curatorial team, curator

Viewers have to engage in a way that does not allow them to just say, 'Well, the past is gone.' We wanted them to reflect on the issues confronting our democracy.

Lauren Segal, HET curatorial team, project manager

CELL TWO – WHO IS A CRIMINAL? Guto Bussab

CELL TWO – WHO IS A CRIMINAL?

A story that typified the dilemma of who would be represented in the exhibition was the story of the two Jacks. The first Jack we interviewed was a Pan African Congress stalwart who was arrested in 1960 as part of the anti-pass campaign that led to the Sharpeville massacre. He remembered his time in Number Four with a sense of pride. The second Jack is a man who had spent most of his adult life behind prison bars. He started off his prison career as a delinquent and petty thief and was later imprisoned for murder.

Steve Kwena Mokwena, HET curatorial team, curator

We decided to put up a series of 'mugshots' and ask the visitor to decide 'who is a criminal?' We needed to find a creative solution for how to exhibit Jack the political activist next to Jack the murderer without belittling the former or exonerating the latter. So we get the visitor to weigh each other's crimes up against the reality of how black men were imprisoned, and to make their own judgements. I think this is the most successful intervention we have done, because it embodies our principles of interactivity and critical engagement.

Mark Gevisser, HET curatorial team, content

ABLUTIONS

There were two ablution areas in the prison
courtyard. Sparse quotes give the visitor
a sense of forced humiliations and violence
around the toilets.

THE ABLUTIONS AREA Guto Bussab

This is the area in the jail where food was delivered in large metal drums. Black prisoners received inferior food to that of white or coloured prisoners and food was used as a form of trade and currency.

TAUSA

For a long time, Drum editor, Anthony Sampson, and photographer, Bob Gosani, had been looking for ways to photograph prisons. They eventually identified a building that overlooks Number Four. As a black man, Gosani could not simply enter the building so a white friend, Deborah Duncan, posed as a photographer and told the building superintendent that she wanted to take panoramic shots of Johannesburg with her assistants, Bob Gosani and Arthur Maimane. Duncan kept the superintendent busy while Gosani captured images of the tausa dance in the Number Four courtyard with a powerful telephoto lens.

Sharon Cort, HET curatorial team, researcher

THE *TAUSA* Bob Gossani, Bailey's African History Archive

You have a choice when you get a very powerful image like the *tausa*. If we'd blown it up large, people might say, 'Oh my God! Isn't that the most awful thing?' Sometimes an experience like that can also nullify the subtlety of other responses. I liked the idea of making the viewer active rather than making it all terribly easy. So the visitor has to walk to this quite small, subtle image and then realise the horror of it.

Clive van den Berg, HET curatorial team, designer

THE *TAUSA* EXHIBITION Guto Bussab

POWER AND PUNISHMENT

I had been searching unsuccessfully for prison artefacts for months. In desperation, I decided to travel to prisons in other parts of the country. I went to a place called Willowvale in the former Transkei. To my amazement, I found this flogging frame. It was covered by grass and we had to literally pull it out. I also found lots of prison blankets, shoes and uniforms in these rural areas. All the stuff I found was signed off to be destroyed and we were just lucky to be there in time to rescue it.

The flogging frame, which was in operation until the mid-1980s, is a powerful symbol of the brutality of the system. It is imposing in the cell and while it gives you a sense of the viciousness of the system, you also hear prisoner testimonies of gang violence.

Churchill Madikida, HET curatorial team, collections

You must give them cigarettes if you have them.

CELL 3 – POWER AND PUNISHMENT Guto Bussab

CELL FOUR – RESISTANCE AND RESILIENCE Guto Bussab

CELL FOUR – RESISTANCE AND RESILIENCE

The blanket and soap sculptures show how prisoners preserved their dignity and found creative ways to amuse themselves and hold on to their spirit. The sculptures were created by two ex-prisoners, Isaac Luphindo and Vusi Tshabalala, for the exhibition. They are typical of those that were made by prisoners every Sunday. Prisoners with the most creatively decorated cell would win privileges for a week - a baked cake from the kitchen or an extra slice of bread each day. The blanket sculptures were also made by 'underlings' in the cell as a way of pleasing the cell bosses. The couches were offered as a form of comfort for the cell bosses.

Churchill Madikida, HET curatorial team, collections

These things reminded us of the world outside the prison walls, the life we left behind and the things we longed for.

Vusi Tshabalala, ex-prisoner and blanket sculptor

We used blankets for recreation. We turned them into ludo boards with bits of toilet paper serving as markers. We also made carvings using soap and paper as another way of passing the time.

Vusi Tshabalala, ex-prisoner and blanket sculptor

SOAP SCULPTURES BY VUSI TSHABALALA Guto Bussab

EMAKHULUKHUTHU – THE ISOLATION CELLS

EMAKHULUKHUTU – ISOLATION CELLS WITH THE EXHIBITION IMAGES OF THE GRAFFITI ON THE DOORS Guto Bussab

In Number Four, you walk under an observation bridge, which makes me feel like I'm in a Nazi concentration camp, and down into what really is the darkest place in the darkness of the prison: the solitary punishment cells. Like everything else in Number Four, it is built around an outdoor courtyard. But in this punishment section, the outdoor courtyard has wire mesh between you and the sky. So you're outside but you're caged. Coming off this courtyard are the cell doors and on the back of them, is the graffiti scratched into the metal door by the prisoners. And what's fascinating about them is that a lot of the people who were kept there were not necessarily political yet the discourse on the doors is a discourse of liberation - Viva ANC etc. The liberation struggle became a metaphor for freedom. You're incarcerated, you're oppressed by white warders, you identify with the liberation struggle.

Mark Gevisser, HET curatorial team, content

Some of the people being punished in these cells were migrant workers from other parts of the continent. When I read their graffiti this sense of forlornness comes over me. They were enmeshed in a brutal system so far away from home, all they could do was scratch their names and where they came from on the doors of that dark, dark place. I kept trying to imagine what they would've liked people to know about them and their lives.

Audrey Brown, HET curatorial team, content

GUARD HOUSE IN FRONT OF THE ISOLATION CELLS Andrew Meintjes

THE RESPONSE ROOM

The curatorial principle of encouraging participation and facilitating public ownership of the Hill found expression in the response room. Here, the process of making the exhibition was displayed – both to show the behind-the-scenes workings of the team and as an invitation to visitors and ex-prisoners to leave their responses to add another layer to the story of Constitution Hill.

This room is a very important last stop for visitors. It is the place where they can reflect on what they have seen and heard and also record their responses. We have placed a 'dignity book' next to one of the old prison registers from Number Four. In here, we invite ex-prisoners to inscribe their names – this time out of choice – so as to create a record of as many of the ex-prisoners who are still alive as possible. It is very exciting and gratifying to watch the list of names growing over the months.

Lauren Segal, HET curatorial team, project manager

For the men who survived Number Four and shared their memories here as free men, the pain may not go away. But, as harvesters of their stories, we hope the exhibition goes some way towards ridding future generations of the dark spell of prisons like Number Four. As one of the men told us, 'It's here where they trampled on our rights and it is here that hope is coming alive...I am no longer afraid to walk past the old Fort. I want my children to know what happened inside here.'

Steve Kwena Mokwena, HET curatorial team, curator

ARCHIVE DRAWERS OF EX-PRISONER AND WARDER WORKSHOP PHOTOGRAPHS Guto Bussab

I am honoured to declare the new Constitutional Court building at Number One Constitution Hill open. May it be a shining beacon of hope for the protection of human rights and the advancement of human dignity and liberty.

President Thabo Mbeki, 21 March 2004

Inaugurating The Court

21 March 2004

The Opening

The Constitutional Court building was inaugurated on Human Rights Day, 21 March 2004. Judges, politicians and dignitaries from South Africa and abroad gathered in front of the new Court. The calm on the day belied the frantic efforts of the past weeks to get the site ready. The teams involved shared a moment of great relief when, under clear blue skies, Chief Justice Arthur Chaskalson led the judges onto the podium and opened the proceedings. Speeches from Gauteng Premier, Mbhazima Shilowa, and President Thabo Mbeki followed. And then, amidst tears and laughter, twenty-seven children born in 1994, South Africa's first year of democracy, recited the Bill of Rights in the eleven official languages. President Mbeki declared the Court open and, together with the Chief Justice, led the guests into the new building.

This beautiful building, which is now the Court's home, stands where once a bastion of white power and oppression stood. It is appropriate that a landmark of our largest city should no longer be a prison; that in its place should be a court, which is a symbol of our democracy.

Chief Justice Arthur Chaskalson, 21 March 2004

The Court represents the conversion of the negative, hateful energy of colonialism, subjugation and oppression into a positive, hopeful energy for the present and the future; a celebration of the creative potential of our people that has given us an architectural jewel. Constitution Hill also makes the statement that central Johannesburg will continue to grow and thrive, no longer a place of segregation and urban decay, but a leader in our country and continent as the city of the future.

President Thabo Mbeki, 21 March 2004

PRESIDENT THABO MBEKI MAKING THE KEYNOTE ADDRESS Oscar G

top GAUTENG PREMIER MBHAZIMA SHILOWA, FORMER SPEAKER OF THE HOUSE OF ASSEMBLY FRENE GINWALA, PRESIDENT THABO MBEKI AND
CHIEF JUSTICE ARTHUR CHASKALSON OUTSIDE THE FRONT DOORS OF THE CONSTITUTIONAL COURT
bottom CHIEF JUSTICE ARTHUR CHASKALSON GREETS GUESTS   Oscar G

The Court

This is not a single building, but a collection of individual components making up a bigger entity. The building mirrors the South African story where the population, the languages, the provinces and different identities come together to be one.

Janina Masojada, Andrew Makin and Paul Wygers, architects

The potency of the Court's design lies in its fragmentation of the architectural languages of power.

Hannah le Roux, Art South Africa, volume two, winter 2004

THE CONSTITUTIONAL COURT AT NIGHT Angela Buckland

The Foyer

THE COURT FOYER Guto Bussab

The Court foyer and chamber are at the top of the site and are located as the primary focus of Constitution Square. The emblem that we used for the foyer was 'justice under a tree'. In our society, the shade of the tree is used as a place of communal gathering, whether for school, meetings of a community with their elders or simple social exchange. The translation of this into physical form is through the pillars that lean at angles that mimic the trunks of trees under which visitors can sit. The columns gather around a clearing, making space. They stand alone, in pairs and in groups, as we would. The foyer is occupied even when empty.

Janina Masojada, Andrew Makin and Paul Wygers, architects

When you ask me about my favourite spot, I just want to tell you the foyer in the Court. I grew up in a very traditional setting where every time there were quarrels within families, they would go and report to the traditional leader and then he'd summon elders and they would sit down under the tree. The foyer, which is modelled on the idea of these *lekgotlas* or *kgoros*, allows me explain everything to visitors about African justice under the tree which I grew up with. It is good that it is very visible in the Court.

Lebogang Mogalaka, tour guide

The architects were inspired in their design of the lobby by this woodcut, Making Democracy Work by Sandile Goje.

People who come to the Court
will not be left wondering why
we need a constitution.

Albie Sachs, Constitutional Court judge

The Court Chamber

I firmly believe that Courts must work in public: that the doors must be open, not as a hollow gesture, but so people can see what's happening. The law is a prophylactic, a diffuser of tensions. I make it a hobby when I get into a town to go and sit in the back of a Magistrate's Court and you can't see or hear anything. This Court's chamber is unique. People can come in and see and hear what the judges are saying. It is amazing.

Johann Kriegler, former Constitutional Court judge

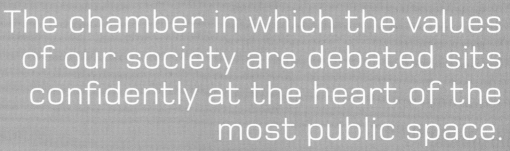

The chamber in which the values
of our society are debated sits
confidently at the heart of the
most public space.

Janina Masojada, Andrew Makin and Paul Wygers, architects

THE CONSTITUTIONAL COURT IN SESSION Guto Bussab

The Library

The library, the repository of knowledge, is at the bottom
of the slope of the site, at the opposite end from the foyer
and chamber. It is designed as the tallest form on the side
of the ridge as a glowing beacon. At the north end of the
building is this beacon of knowledge – and at the south, the
chamber of wisdom.

Janina Masojada, Andrew Makin and Paul Wygers, architects

The library is the hub of the building. This is where the
judges and the law clerks conduct their research. They look
at best practices from around the world so that they can
produce their judgements. We have a very good collection
of international and comparative law. With the launch of
the virtual library we are making this wonderful resource
available to a wider community.

Sheryl Luthuli, chief librarian

left **LIBRARY INTERIOR** Guto Bussab *right* **LIBRARY EXTERIOR** Andrew Meintjes

The Judges' Chambers

The judges' chambers are located in the internal courtyard of the building, attached to the western side of the building as fingers, with water and garden rooms between them. They are the most private components of the building.

Janina Masojada, Andrew Makin and Paul Wygers, architects

Judges are used to stark wooden panel walls, hefty furniture, red carpets. But now we have introduced personality, colour and character into the judges' chambers and into their working lives. This is where I am all day long for maybe five, six days a week. It is a wonderful, stimulating environment. I love coming here.

Yvonne Mokgoro, Constitutional Court judge

Do I like working in the building? I love it. It's beautiful. It's wood, steel and glass. The beauty of the building is an endorsement of the beauty of constitutionality. It emphasises so many core values.

Johann Kriegler, former Constitutional Court judge

It is nice to work here. At the old building, we never used to see each other. Here, we can see each other through the windows because they are all open. It has brought us together in new ways and brought an interaction between us secretaries. We are now able to communicate much more easily.

Elizabeth Moloto, secretary to Judge O'Regan

top **THE JUDGES' CHAMBERS INTERIOR** Guto Bussab *bottom* **THE JUDGES' CHAMBERS EXTERIOR** Andrew Meintjes

There are six materials used in the building. Concrete, timber, steel, stone and glass are found all over. But the one I love the most is light. It exists all over and cannot be placed. It connects the building to the world outside. It is the spiritual and emotional heart of the building.

Albie Sachs, Constitutional Court judge

For us, it is important to see how the past has been translated into the current language of contemporary design – the mosaics, the colours, the artwork. It's amazing to see how a space and the light can influence your feelings and emotions.

Anika Grobler, design lecturer, Nelson Mandela Metropolitan University, Port Elizabeth

INTERIOR OF THE FOYER AND THE JUDGES' LOUNGE Guto Bussab

LIGHT–FILLED COURT FOYER Guto Bussab

The Integrated Artwork

I don't know of any project that has garnered contributions from such a wide range of people from such a diversity of cultural and training backgrounds. The intention is that people from all over our country can come to the building and find something that they can identify with. There are many hands that have made this building.

Janina Masojada, architect

THE SHUTTERS ALONG THE GREAT AFRICAN STEPS BY LEWIS LEVIN AND PATRICK RORKE Guto Bussab
GATE FOR JUDGE'S CHAMBER BY LISA PEROLD Brian Orlin
MOSAICS IN THE COURT FOYER BY JANE DU RAND Brian Orlin

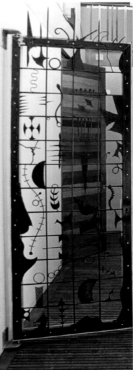

This was my first project for a public building of this kind.
I was so honoured to become part of building the Court.
I feel like I have contributed to the history of South Africa.
The process was very difficult, working on such large pieces.
I haven't seen my chandeliers hanging but I hope to come to
Johannesburg soon and see them outside the Court.

Lindelani Ngwenya, wire sculptor

The building is marked by a number of defining features; some inspired, others
markedly kitsch. Of the latter, the Court's numerous artistic finishes rank as
questionable. They sometime read as embellishments, too decorative, and could
be viewed as whimsical. Not all have integrated well into the building.

Sean O'Toole, editor of Art South Africa

COPPER COURT CHAMBER DOOR BY ANDREW LINDSAY, MYRA FASSLER KAMSTRA, VERNA JOOSTE, MARK ZAMMIT, LARRY DE KLERK Andrew Meintjes
HAND WOVEN CARPETS BY SIPHIWE ZULU Guto Bussab
FRONT DOORS OF THE CONSTITUTIONAL COURT DESIGNED BY ANDREW VERSTER, ANDRIES BOTHA, LINDELANI C NDINISA, MUSA NGCOBO,
SMANGA MADLALA, DUMISANI MTHETHWA, JABULANI MKHIZE, ERNEST MTHETHWA, RICHARD MAPHUMULO, RICHARD SHANGE Guto Bussab

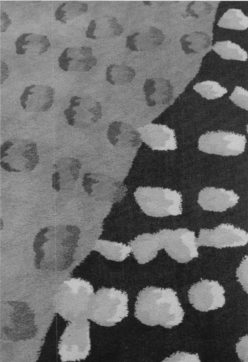

The We The People Wall

At the opening ceremony of the Court, each guest was asked to write a message of hope to be engraved on a copper plate that would form part of the We The People Wall on Constitution Square. Every year on Human Rights Day, handwritten messages from visitors to Constitution Hill will be engraved on copper and added to the wall, providing a people's record of the first twenty-five years of the site. Visitors were also interviewed about their first impressions of the Hill.

> I congratulate you for what the people of South Africa have achieved. From the ashes of oppression, you have sprung a monument of hope. And hope is what should spur you on to the everlasting future.
>
> *Mr Justice Lewanika, Chief Justice from Zambia*

I am thrilled by the precinct because of the way in which it combines history and the future. I do not think there is a place anywhere in the world where you combine scenes of brutality with visions of the future. I think it will be a great tourist attraction for years to come.

George Bizos, advocate

MESSAGES ON THE WE THE PEOPLE WALL Guto Bussab

The Hoarding

At the time of the opening of the Court, the Women's Jail was still under construction. The new offices were being built in the northern courtyard to house the Commission on Gender Equality as well as other Chapter Nine organisations. But it was critically important that the presence of the Women's Jail be felt at the ceremony. Images of several of the women ex-prisoners were mounted on the building hoardings on the western side of the site.

↘

CHAPTER NINE ORGANISATIONS

Chapter Nine organisations are statutory institutions set out in Chapter Nine of the Constitution which support and monitor constitutional democracy. They include the Office of the Public Protector; the South African Human Rights Commission; the Commission for the Promotion and Protection of the Rights of Cultural, Religious and Linguistic Communities; the Commission on Gender Equality; the Auditor General and the Independent Electoral Commission.

IMAGES OF WOMEN EX-PRISONERS ON THE HOARDING OF CONSTITUTION SQUARE Brian Orlin

Responses

Few buildings in the world have produced such an enthusiastic response. Judges, architects and visitors to the Court have all praised the building's aesthetic appeal and its truly South African character. A handful of commentators have cautioned that the idealism of the building may not weather the test of time.

The building is magnificent, imaginative, inspiring, life-enhancing; a vindication of careful, gifted design.

Alan Lipman, writer and architectural critic

Much of this idealism of the building is, of course, untested. The regenerative potential of the development still has to prove itself. As such, cynics might determine hints of hubris in the high-minded statements explaining the Court's function. After all, Johannesburg's urban landscape offers telling examples of architectural impositions that bear no parity between intent and outcome.

Sean O'Toole, editor of Art South Africa

I've been to the Supreme Court in America and the High Court in London. They're wonderful edifices, the grandeur and the sheer volume, but they're very domineering and dominating. And the justice feels quite oppressive, which I don't feel here. Here, it's 'We, the people'.

Neil Fraser, former executive director, CJP

The building is open and airy and transparent. We see in it a symbol of the openness and accessibility we aim to ensure at the Court. This is in stark contrast with the past, when people went to court only under duress.

Pius Langa, Chief Justice of the Constitutional Court

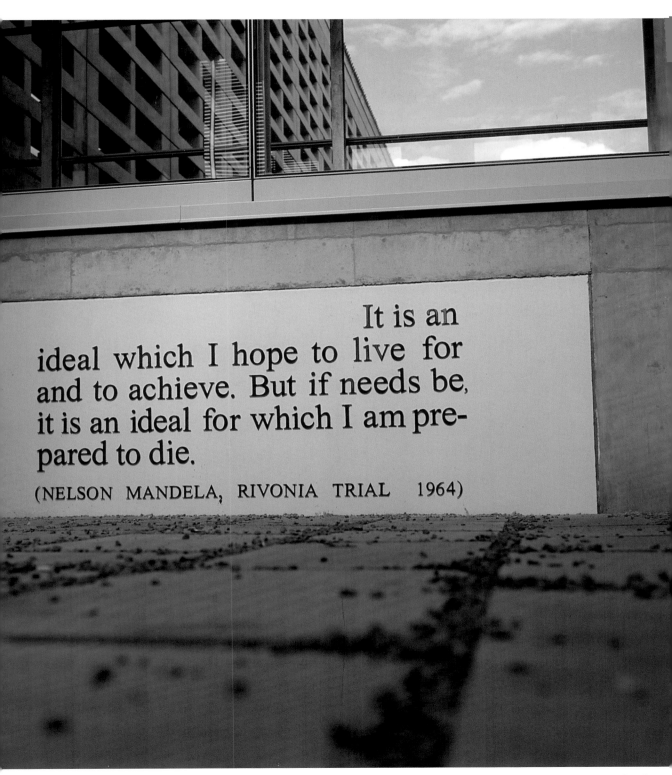

It is an ideal which I hope to live for and to achieve. But if needs be, it is an ideal for which I am pre-pared to die.

(NELSON MANDELA, RIVONIA TRIAL   1964)

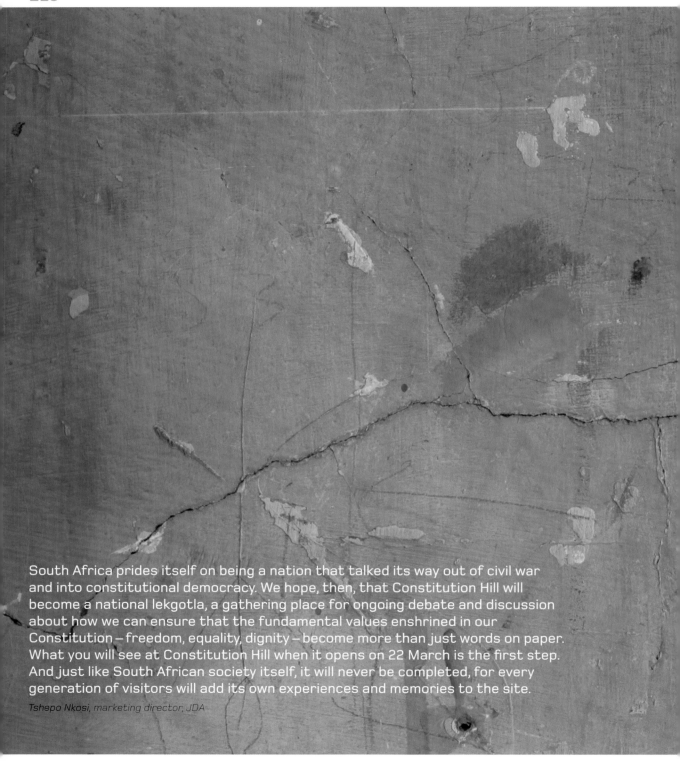

South Africa prides itself on being a nation that talked its way out of civil war and into constitutional democracy. We hope, then, that Constitution Hill will become a national lekgotla, a gathering place for ongoing debate and discussion about how we can ensure that the fundamental values enshrined in our Constitution—freedom, equality, dignity—become more than just words on paper. What you will see at Constitution Hill when it opens on 22 March is the first step. And just like South African society itself, it will never be completed, for every generation of visitors will add its own experiences and memories to the site.

Tshepo Nkosi, marketing director, JDA

The Public Arrive

22 March 2004

Constitution Hill Opens

In the months leading up to 22 March 2004, a team worked day and night to hire and train staff that could run the heritage, education and tourism programmes and deal with the daily operations of the large mixed-use heritage precinct of Constitution Hill.

There was no model to follow. There was not a large pool of people trained in this to draw on. But the mission of the Hill inspired our team to work above and beyond the time we had at our disposal. We made it happen in the end because we were personally committed to what it represented. I don't know of any other museum in the world that has gotten up and running in such a short space of time.

Amy Kaufman, LORD Cultural Resources

After the big push to open and the initial celebrations died down, there was still no time to rest. We had to fully train staff that was new to the complexities of operating a heritage site of this size. It was time to develop unique initiatives to introduce Constitution Hill to the people of South Africa and the world beyond. It was time to complete the myriad construction finishes and attend to the many details that were lost in the opening days. The opening had preceded the dress rehearsal!

Susan Dunlop, LORD Cultural Resources

There were strenuous moments. There were tantrums. There was also a lot of laughter. We had protracted meetings with the judges, the JDA and the HET team sitting around the table thrashing out the issues. But we always ended on a positive note because we all ultimately realised that we needed to see the lighter side and not get bogged down in the mountain of details.

Tshepo Nkosi, marketing director, JDA

BASE OF THE GREAT AFRICAN STEPS BETWEEN NUMBER FOUR AND THE CONSTITUTIONAL COURT Gisele Wulfsohn

The Tour Guides

The opening of the Visitors' Centre and the start of the tours of the Hill signalled an exciting new chapter for the site as a tourist destination in the inner city of Johannesburg. The group of newly trained young guides was recruited mainly from neighbourhoods around the site. During the training process, it emerged that a significant number of the guides had parents or relatives who had been imprisoned at Number Four and had grown up hearing stories of the jails. It was exciting to see a passion for the project emerge amongst the guides. It was equally exciting to witness the Hill becoming a platform for economic development. Fifteen youngsters were now trained and had jobs at the Hill.

My grandfather was imprisoned here in the fifties for the pass laws. I have memories of him talking about this place as I was growing up. When I told him what I was doing, he exclaimed, 'You are working at the very same Old Fort which was used as a prison?' I told him that the place is no longer a prison, that it is now being used for heritage. He lives in Limpopo but he says that he would like to come and visit the Hill and have me as his guide.

Clement Masemola, tour guide

Two of my uncles were held in Number Four. They are old now, living in the rural areas. But being a young man and relating these stories now as a guide really touches me. The first time I did the tour, I nearly cried. I can say I've been summoned as a guide. I'm a messenger. We say 'Ke Morongwa' in Northern Sotho. It feels like a privilege to work here. It means a lot to me.

Lebogang Mogalaka, tour guide

My Grandmother came here to Johannesburg a long time ago and worked as a domestic. She used to tell me stories of how she would come here to bail out her friends and former boyfriend. It felt amazing when I brought her back and she told me all about the spaces.

Lungile Ndlovu, tour guide

top MOSES NGWENYA LEADING A GROUP OF TOURISTS UP THE RAMPART STEPS, *middle* JUDGE ALBIE SACHS LEADING A TOUR GROUP ON CONSTITUTION SQUARE, *bottom* A LEARNER READING THE *TAUSA* PANEL IN NUMBER FOUR Oscar G

My father was imprisoned at Number Four three times.
Until I became a tour guide here, I had no idea of what lurked
behind these foreboding ramparts. It's been a voyage of
discovery for me and I hope to make it a voyage that each
and every South African can take in his or her lifetime.

Dorah Molefe, tour guide

NEWLY OPENED VISITORS' CENTRE WITH BOOKINGS OFFICERS TREVOR CHUEU AND RUTH CELE Guto Bussab

MOSES NGWENYA WITH VISITORS IN FOOD AREA OF NUMBER FOUR

Since I started working as a tour guide, not only have I appreciated what our parents went through, I have begun to truly understand the gift of our freedom.

Johanna Mavhungu, tour guide

VISITORS IN THE WHO IS A CRIMINAL CELL IN NUMBER FOUR Guto Bussab

Visitor Feedback

In the first months after opening, visitor feedback cards showed extremely high levels of visitor satisfaction with the experience. Also impressive was the fact that in the first weeks, at least half of the visitors to the site were from Hillbrow. The host community was embracing Constitution Hill along with the international tourists, students and communnity organisations.

Conscious and mind-liberating, spiritually uplifting.

A unique embodiment of our past, present and future and a world model. Architecture and art is fused with history and politics. Most inspiring and awesome.

Thank you for showing an American how democracy can be successful.

A wonderful place to learn about the past and feel positive about the future.

The learners so enjoyed their visit that we are still getting messages from parents thanking us for bringing them here. The guides were superb and they know what to do. The teachers have decided to make it an annual thing so you will be hearing from me again.

I am so sad it is our history and so proud it is so superbly preserved. Many, many thanks.

This place was extraordinary. It was an excellent experience for us.

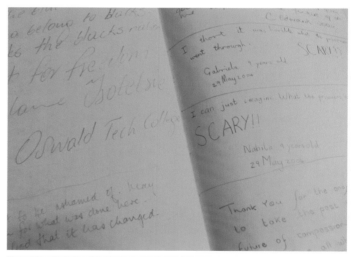

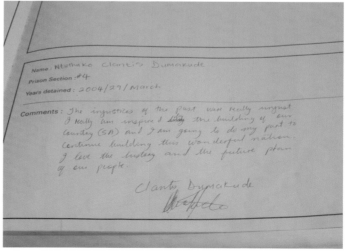

I think this place should be visited by everybody young and old so as to see where we come from, where we are and where we are going.

Astonishing reality of our history & equally astonishing hope for our future. Exceptional place for all to visit.

LUNGILE NDLOVU IN THE RESPONSE ROOM Guto Bussab

Public Programmes

Weeks after the doors of the Hill opened, the new institution began to offer a wide range of public programmes, from school tours to music events and poetry, from small group conversations to large celebrations of important public holidays. The programmes were carefully designed to access new audiences who might not ordinarily visit a heritage site and to ensure that the Hill truly became a living heritage precinct.

The Hill is fast becoming the civic space in the inner city that we dreamed of. Over the last year, it has been increasingly used as a centre for dialogue, debate and dissent around current social issues. It feels like Johannesburg was hungry for a venue of this kind.

Lauren Segal, project manager

There was a very well thought out vision for programmes when I started working here. My task was to bring the ideas that were expressed in the business plan to life. Our key strategy was to approach relevant organisations to use our site for their talks and events. In the beginning, we had to work hard to sell ourselves. Very few people knew who we were. Now we get approached all the time to host programmes. The transformation has been phenomenal.

Danielle Melville, public programmes manager

When I started working here, the education department had no database or links to schools. I set about developing learning materials and talking to the Department of Education, teachers and educational organisations. There were long hours of planning and networking, creating partnerships. Many learners have now toured the Hill and that feels very gratifying.

Thembi Malao, education manager

THE SCREENING OF NINE FILMS BY ARTIST WILLIAM KENTRIDGE AND MUSIC BY PHILIP MILLER IN THE COURTYARD OF THE OLD FORT John Hodgkiss

TOUR GUIDE NKUNZI NKABINDA OUTSIDE THE MANDELA
CELL WITH A GROUP OF LEARNERS Oscar G

Our lekgotla series of informal
conversations has been one of the most
successful programmes. The discussions
have involved ex-prisoners, learners,
teachers, politicians, policymakers,
psychologists and ordinary South Africans.
There have been some amazing encounters,
particularly for the school kids who have
had the opportunity to talk to a whole
range of people.

Thembi Malao, education manager

ONE OF THE FIRST *LEKGOTLAS* WITH EX-PRISONER KHEHLA SHUBANE WHO WAS IMPRISONED IN NUMBER FOUR DURING THE 1976 UPRISING Oscar G

Children's Room Events and Children's Day

The Children's Room was set up in a space in the Old Fort so as to create a dedicated experience for young children and their families at the Hill. The mission of the room is to 'bring to life the Children's Bill of Rights in an African, tactile, fun, interactive and age-appropriate way so that all children can work alongside their families in beginning to understand and experience the bill of rights'.

EX-PRISONER VESTA SMITH SPEAKING IN THE CHILDREN'S ROOM ABOUT HER EXPERIENCES IN THE JAIL Bambanani Professional Photographers

The work I am doing is not about teaching. It is about support, protection. We love this job. It is for the betterment of children. The children are our future.

Mmabatho Mokwena, educator, Children's Room

Children of all ages have come here to play and learn about rights and responsibilities through organised and informal workshops where we use poetry, music and movement. We try to build confidence amongst young people that will enable them to participate in democratic processes in the future.

Smacx Tlali, educator, Children's Room

The room has become a meeting place where privileged groups interact with less privileged groups. The children talk a lot. I think the children appreciate this space. It lights up their faces.

Mmabatho Mokwena, educator, Children's Room

EDUCATORS SMACX TLALI AND MMABATHO MOKWENA RUNNING A PROGRAMME WITH LEARNERS Bambanani Professional Photographers

Temporary Exhibitions

A temporary exhibition space was created in the
former dining room of the Old Fort to accommodate
short-term exhibitions that relate not only to the
Hill's history but to contemporary issues of civic and
social significance.

We have had exhibitions by well-known artists
like Willem Boshoff followed by an exhibition
of photographs of Hillbrow done by students
from the Wits school of architecture. There
is something exciting about running a venue
that can accommodate such diverse shows and
attract very diverse audiences.

Danielle Melville, public programmes manager

TEMPORARY EXHIBITION *GOD SAVE THE QUEEN* (2004) BY WILLEM BOSHOFF Karen Boshoff

The temporary exhibition space has been one of the unexpected successes of the Hill. We originally anticipated only four exhibitions a year. The gallery conditions are very basic and yet artists and organisations from all over are lining up to show their work in a place of social relevance.

Churchill Madikida, exhibition manager

The Opening of the Women's Jail

On the night of 2 August 2005, the Commission on Gender Equality (CGE) officially opened its new offices in the recently completed buildings in the prison's main courtyard. The buildings also housed the regional offices of the Public Protector and the Commission for the Promotion and Protection of Rights of Cultural, Religious and Linguistic Communities. On the same evening, the exhibition in of the old parts of the Women's Jail was opened. In an extraordinary ceremony, women ex-prisoners led the guests in a candlelit procession from Constitution Square to the Women's Jail. Joyce Seroke, an ex-political prisoner and Chairperson of the CGE introduced the evening's proceedings.

top **GUESTS ASSEMBLED ON CONSTITUTION SQUARE** James Outway   *bottom* **GUESTS IN THE WOMEN'S JAIL ATRIUM** James Outway

LABYRINTH IN THE LAUNDRY COURTYARD OF THE WOMEN'S JAIL LIT UP BY THE LANTERNS PLACED
THERE BY EX-PRISONERS AND OTHER GUESTS DURING THE OPENING CEREMONY James Outway

top EX–PRISONERS LEADING THE PROCESSION FROM CONSTITUTION SQUARE TO THE WOMEN'S JAIL
bottom, from left to right ZUBEIDA 'JUBY' MAYET, NIKIWE DEBORAH MATSHOBA, VESTA SMITH, ESTHER BARSEL James Outway

top EX–PRISONERS LEADING THE PROCESSION FROM CONSTITUTION SQUARE TO THE WOMEN'S JAIL
bottom, from left to right NOMSA NTHWETHWA AND SIBONGILE TSHABALA, FATIMA MEER, JOYCE PILISO SEROKE, FORMER POLITICAL PRISONER
AND CHAIRPERSON OF THE COMMISSION ON GENDER EQUALITY, CUTTING THE RIBBON TO OPEN THE JAIL James Outway

The Years Ahead

The opening of the Women's Jail precinct in August 2005 marked the end of the first phase of the site's development. The Court had been built and had been hearing cases in the new court chamber for just over a year. The heritage site had opened and more than 160 000 visitors had come to the exhibitions or attended one of the many events on offer. The Chapter Nine Organisations have taken occupation of the new buildings in the Women's Jail and the precinct is now functioning as a mixed-use interactive heritage space. But there is still a lot more development to come in the next few years.

A new building currently referred to as the Visitors' Centre is being developed directly opposite the Constitutional Court. The Visitors' Centre will house an exhibition that tells the story of the making of our constitutional democracy as well as auditoriums, conference facilities and restaurants. Excitingly, the Mandela Foundation has agreed that the Nelson Mandela Centre of Memory and Commemoration will also be located in this building. This Centre will house Mandela's legacy – his vast archive, his gifts, photographs etc. We are extremely proud of the partnership with the Mandela Foundation and of the opportunity to provide a home for this important initiative at the Hill.

Graeme Reid, former CEO, JDA

The commercial development on the western portion of the site includes plans for a small hotel, retail facilities to serve the needs of visitors as well as office accommodation for tenants who have an interest in human rights and constitution-related matters. The old Queen Victoria Hospital complex and nurses' quarters will be converted into rented flats. This project offers a range of opportunities for investors.

Brian Orlin, development manager, Constitution Hill

A very generous grant will allow us to start preservation and restoration work on the Old Fort. An exhibition will be mounted throughout the building that will tell the military history of the Jail as well as the experiences of white male prisoners who were held in the cells. There will be permanent exhibitions in each of the Jail buildings on site.

Brian Orlin, development manager, Constitution Hill

Reflections...

It's very fulfilling to know that one has been part of this. History has not been forgotten, that is the most important thing.

Nikiwe Deborah Matshoba, ex-political prisoner and researcher

Reflections...

I've taken a couple of thousand people on urban renewal tours through the city. We always end up at Con Hill. I've found lots of people who didn't know it was here. But I've yet to find a person that isn't moved. It's an important catalyst not just in the transformation of the city, but in the transformation of the country and the transformation of the people in the country. Both white and black can be tremendously affected emotionally and psychologically by what's happening here. It's a very important icon.

Neil Fraser, former executive director, Central Johannesburg Partnership

The hardest thing has not been the technical or financial challenges of this project and certainly, we have had those. The hardest thing has been dealing with the passions that everyone has for the project. Every single person who has worked here is touched by the place and has become passionate in some way. The passion has made the Hill what it is today. But it has also created conflicts along the way – everyone wants it to be something because it means so much. This has not been a straightforward construction development.

Brian Orlin, development manager, Constitution Hill

I think there's still quite a distance between Hillbrow and Constitution Hill. The idea of people coming here to hang out and read their newspapers on the way back from work still has to be realised. But these kind of visions will take time to develop. I look forward to seeing a thriving Constitution Square in five years' time.

Nabeel Essa, HET team, architect

I think Constitution Hill has played an enormously important role in opening up the CBD as an incredibly richly textured and interesting place for tourists to explore.

Lucy Kaplan, HET team, tourism

My favourite spot is up the ramparts, because when you're up the ramparts, you get to see almost the whole of Joburg and you feel like you are on a bridge. It's an honour to work in a place like this. I grew up under true apartheid and have witnessed the change to a democratic state. When I walk up onto the ramparts and look out over Constitution Hill and the city, I get a sense that, 'Okay, these terrible things happened but we're going somewhere very exciting.' I feel like I want to shout out, 'Yay! It's happening.'

Churchill Madikida, HET team, collections curator

It is encouraging for me to see how the site has become public space in which South Africans choose to spend time because it inspires a vision for the future.

Sharon Cort, HET team, researcher

Listening to the ex-prisoners is something that I treasure in my life. Symbolically, it is powerful to have the Constitutional Court here – it's the best thing that could happen to this space. But the danger is assuming that that it is enough. For me this place is about the people that went through these prisons and their families. The challenge is to make this a place where Africans can congregate and say, 'This is where our suffering came from, this is where our freedom came from.' It needs to function in this way and also as a tourism site.

Thapelo Joy Pelo, HET team, oral history

This is a project that makes you wake up screaming in the middle of the night, because there's a huge amount to worry about. But now that it is open, the place has a life of its own. It's bigger than any of the role-players. It's about an idealisation of what we might be. It's aspirational. Ask yourself this: 'How lucky do you have to be, to be in the right place at the right time, to be able to put together something where you build a building like the Constitutional Court?' You design a site, you get to engage in debates and the delivery of an interpretation of this hugely important prison complex. You have to be hugely lucky to be in the right place at the right time.

Graeme Reid, former CEO, JDA

PANORAMIC VIEW OF THE SITE Andrew Meintjes

We the People Messages

What a wonderful creation in the History of S.A. especially after 1994 general elections. 'I feel very safe by saying that the previously existed structure to infringe on human rights at large has now been restructured, renovated and transformed not only to look nicer, but to assist the whole S.A inhabitants in enjoying the advanced, non-sexist and non-racial judgement that never existed in this building "PREVIOUSLY".

Constable J. P. Mapowya
SAPS Hillbrow
Station Youth-Co-ordinator.

TRIUMPH
IN
TRANSCENDENCE

Edwin Cameron
21 March 2004

The New South Africa has brought lots of opportunities for us youth.

I'm 17 years old, and I have things that my grand-parents never had.

South Africa has changed, but I think that it still needs a lot of work. It will get to what our leaders wanted it to be. I like to thank Nelson Mandela, Mo Sisulu, and Mo Thambo for giving us what we have today.

REBECCA POGISO CHOMA
03/03/04

This place is a bookend for my life... for our lives in South Africa. It is at the beginning and at the end of our constitution. It is at the beginning and the end of our quest for reconciliation. It is a place that says we have arrived... but it is a place from which our journey our hope for justice, begins again.

Graeme Simpson.

Gay People Should be Considered as human beings not animals.

lets not go through what we went ~~through in the~~ during the aparteid separating black from white so do not separate homosexual from heterosexual.

The South African Constitution is to my limited knowledge one of the best in the world, therefore there is no turning back. This country must move on. We must find men and women with true vision, who will lead it, filled with hope, to an understanding of the future where corruption, racism and nepotism will have no place.

Nesta Smith

17/02/2004

CONSTITUTIONAL HILL - MADE ME TO RECONCIL WITH THE OLD APARTY REGIME, BECAUSE I WAS ONE OF THE VICTIM, WHO WHERE DETAINED IN TO FORD FOR GROUP AREA'S ACT. SO TO BUILD IT, IT BROUGHT OUR DIGNITY BACK & CONFORT US AT THE SAME TIME. I ADMIRE THE PERSON OR STRUCTURE THAT CAME WITH THE IDEA OF BUILDING CONSTITUITIONAL HILL. MESSAGE FROM
SARAH SEMATLANE

Information

Team from the JDA
Graeme Reid (CEO), Brian Orlin (Development Manager),
Felicity Human (Development Coordinator), Tshepo Nkosi
(Marketing Director), Agmat Badat (Development Manager),
Vijay Moodley (Development Coordinator), Mohale Mopai
(Development Coordinator)

Team for the Construction of the Court
Architects and Principle Agent – OMM Design Workshops
and Urban Solutions
Quantity Surveyors – Hamlyn Gebhardt, Koor Dindar
Structural Engineers – Arup (Pty) Ltd, Sibanye Consulting
Engineers Joint Venture
Electrical Engineers – VBI Projects
Mechanical Engineers – Arup (Pty) Ltd, Toon Herman &
Associates
Acoustic Engineers – Acusolve
Landscape Architects – African Environmental Design

Main Contractor:
Rainbow Construction – WBHO Joint Venture

Team for the Construction of the Women's Jail
Architects – Kate Otten Architects
Project managers – Holicki and Associates
Quantity Surveyors – Bham, Tayob, Khan and Matunda
Civil /Structural Engineers – Calibre Consulting
Mechanical/Electrical Engineers – Campbell Davies
Consulting Engineers
Fire Protection Consultants – Dynamic Fire Solutions

Main Contractor:
Rainbow Construction

Team for the Relocation of the Mortuary
Architects – JAM Architects
Project Managers – Platynum, Calibre Joint Venture
Quantity Surveyors – Letchmiah, Daya and Mandindi
Civil /Structural Engineers – Calibre Consulting
Mechanical Engineers – Van Zyl and De Villiers Consulting
Engineers
Electrical Engineers – Somiah and Associates
Fire Protection Consultants – Cheinera Fire Consultant

Main Contractor:
Makhudu Barrow Construction

Team for Repairs and Renovation (R&R)
Architects – JAM Architects
Project Managers/Quantity Surveyors – Platynum, Calibre
Joint Venture
Civil /Structural Engineers – Calibre Consulting
Mechanical Engineers – Van Zyl and De Villiers Consulting
Engineers
Electrical Engineers – Somiah and Associates

Construction Management:
Makhudu Barrow Construction

Team for the Construction of the Infrastructure
Architects/Urban Designers – OMM Design Workshop and
Urban Solutions
Project Managers – Arup Development and Planning
Quantity Surveyors – Hamlyn Gebhardt, Koor Dindar
Civil Engineers – Arup, Goba Moahloli & Assoc., and Matla Consultants JV
Structural Engineers – Arup, Sibanye Consulting Engineers JV
Mechanical Engineers – Charles Pein, Khatima Consulting Engineers
Electrical Engineers – VBI Projects, Emzanzi JV
Fire Protection Consultants – Dynamic Fire Solutions
Wet Services – DSB Consulting Engineers
Landscape Architects – African Environmental Design

Main Contractors:
Phase One Infrastructure – Nyoni Projects cc;
Kotze Street Upgrade – Nyoni Projects cc, BT Monareng Contractors
Hospital Street Upgrade –Basotha Managa Construction
Super Basement Bulk Earthworks and Lateral Support – Esor, Franki
Joint Venture
Super basement Main Contract – Nare, Grinaker Joint Venture
Phase Two Infrastructure – WBHO Civils

HET Advisory Group
Graeme Reid (JDA), Tshepo Nkosi (JDA) and Brian Orlin (JDA), Andile
Mahlalutye (Blue IQ), Graeme Simpson and Tracy Viennings (Centre
for the Study of Violence and Reconciliation), Liz Delmont (Heritage
Department at Wits University), Jacque Stoltz, (Gauteng Tourism),
Herbert Prins (Heritage Architect), Peter Stark (Centre for Cultural
Policy and Management, University of Northumbria)

Overall Business Development and Project Management for HET
Ochre Communications: Stan Joseph, Gavin Stafford, Lauren Segal,
Ngaire Blakenberg, Lucy Kaplan
LORD Cultural Resources: Gail Lord, Amy Kaufman, Susan Dunlop

International Consultants
Ralph Applebaum (Ralph Applebaum and Associates), Gail Lord, (LORD
Cultural Resources), Alvin Rosenbaum

Team for the HET team for the Feasibility Study and Business Plan
Dhianaraj Chetty, Stan Joseph, Lauren Segal, Gavin Stafford, Mark
Gevisser, Terry Kurgan, Nina Cohen, Sharon Cort, Nabeel Essa, Lucy
Kaplan, David Cort, Emelia Potenza, Zanele Nkosi, Ann Kushlik, Thapelo Joy
Pelo, Levern Engel, Ereshnee Naidoo, Pshwane Mpa

WSSD exhibition team
Mark Gevisser, Sharon Cort, Lauren Segal, Nina Cohen, Terry Kurgan,
Nabeel Essa, Gail Behrmann, Ashwell Adriaan, Lavern Engel

Curatorial workshop
Thapelo Joy Pelo, Ngaire Blankenburg, Rory Bester, Julia Charlton, Nina
Cohen, Bongi Ndhlomo, Nabeel Essa, Mark Gevisser, Terry Kurgan, Sandy

Prosalendis, Fiona Rankin-Smith, Lauren Segal, and Clive van den Berg

Exhibition Team for Number Four
Steve Kwena Mokwena, Mark Gevisser, Clive van den Berg, Sharon Cort, Lauren Segal, Thapelo Joy Pelo, Audrey Brown, Churchill Madikida, Ngaire Blankenberg, Nabeel Essa, Gavin Stafford, Allison Christie, Isaac Luphindo, Vusi Tshabalala, Sean Slemon, Catherine Muller, Michelle Constance, Phil Bonner, Kate Mooney, Nicole Isaacs, Vincent Truter, Carina Comrie, Adele Prins, Noma Radebe, Carol Liknaitzky

The Exhibition Team for Women's Jail
Lauren Segal, Clive van den Berg, Steve Kwena Mokwena, Audrey Brown, Mark Gevisser, Sharon Cort, Gavin Stafford, Churchill Madikida, Nikiwe Deborah Matshoba, Allison Christie, Catherine Muller, Bronwyn Berry, Michelle Constance, Karen Schoonbee, Tatiana Ferreira, Sandy Shoolman, Gege Leme, Hazel Ngwana, Kate Mooney, Justin Fiske, Luli Callinicos

Implementation Team for the creation of the Institution
Duncan Shelwell, Janine Strong, Lucy Kaplan, Amy Kaufman, Susan Dunlop

Marketing Team
Rob Muirhead, Rafiq Asmal, Soozi van der Linde, Emma Chittenden, Heather Farquharson

We The People
Karima Effendi, Tatiana Ferreira, Adam Broomberg, Oliver Chanarin, Mickey Fonseca, President Kapa

Funders for HET
Atlantic Philanthropies, Ford Foundation, Kellogg Foundation, Mott Foundation, Conference Workshop and Cultural Initiatives, Open Society

Constitution Hill Staff
Jimmy Monisi, Thembi Malao, Danielle Melville, Sharon Premchund, Amy Kaufman, Churchill Madikida, Smacx Tlali, Mmabatho Mokwena, Mpho Germinah Nkadimeng, Wonderboy Peters, Randall Tsolo, Cheryl Stevens, Charley Cain, Gift Monama, Gustav Chuene, Mpho Seoposengwe, Taryn Cohn, Tokello Poho, Trevor Chueu, Valery Ramokgopa, Bongiswa Kota, Bra Sol Setlako, Clement Masemola, David Maziba, Lebo Selao, Lebogang Mogalaka, Lorraine Majola, Lovejoy Mabuza, Lungile Ndlovu, Moses Ngwenya, Ruth Cele, Solly Shishenge, Thando Mashiya, Tshepiso Timbane, Zandile Nkabinde, Valery Ramokgopoa, Nthabiseng Mashike, Sibusiso Ntombelo, Cheryl Stevens, Chioma Onukogu, Matshepo Tlali, Nkunzi Zandile Nkabinde, Obakeng Ramorola, Nthabiseng Mashike

Ex-prisoners that have been identified to date
Albertina Nontsikelelo Sisulu, Lilian Masediba Ngoyi, Nomathemba Funani, Margaret Kriel, Rose Schlachler, Yetta Barenblatt, Getrude Kohn, Pixie Benjamin, Winnie Dadoo, Sylvia Neame, Florence Duncan, Stephanie Kemp, Esther Barsel, Jean Middleton, Ann Nicholson, Shanti Naidoo, Leslie Spiller, Fatima Meer, Vesta Smith, Jeannie Noel, Violet Weinberg, Sheila Weinberg, Elizabeth Letooane, Cecilie Palmer, Sally Motlana, Mathabo Pharase, Rebecca Musi, Winnie Madikizela–Mandela, Betty du Toit, Shalamuth Muller, Nikiwe Deborah Matshoba, Maleshane 'Mally' Mokoena, Mmagauta A Molefe, Sibongile Kubeka, Oshadi Mangena-Phakathi, Palesa Musa, Ellen Nyamende, Thandi Modise, Felicity Human, Sharon Basson, Haanchen Koornhof, Barbara Hogan, Rita Ndzanga, Joyce Piliso Seroke, Mapitso Lolo Tabane, Thenjiwe Mthintso, Rica Hodgson, Hilda Bernstein, Myrtle Berman, Molly Fischer, Trudy Gelb, Maggie Resha, Sheila Hurwitz, Nomakhaya 'Kayo' Ethel Mafuna, Rebecca Musi, Ellen Kuzwayo, Zubeida 'Juby' Mayet, Baby Tyawa, Thandi Zulu, Nomsa Masuku, Joyce Dipale, Nomsa Mthethwa, Gladys Dladla, Evelyn Kealetse, Palesa Musa, Sarah Sematlane, Puleng Ntlaleng, Johanna Nkomo, Yvonne Ntonto Mhlauli, Sepati More, Sibongile Mkhabela, Bella Dlamini, Helen Joseph, Jack Mabaso, Jeffrey Mgiba, Calvin Gabadi, Allen Vusi Radebe, Johnny Mahlaba, William Thelela, Jabulani Madonsela, Sipho Sibiya, Sipho Nkosi, William Mathebula, Sipho Mothibe, Willington Rorwana, Edwin Maluleke, Alphen Ntimbane, Amos Nkosi, Fumasi Masuku, Cornelius Motsumi Mpshe (Manoto), Isaac Hlatshwayo, Thomas Mndaniso, John Moketsi Mahapa, David Maseko, Edward Sonnyboy Bhengu, Paul Lukhele, Ezekiel Mafori Motimele, Peter Moeketsi, Victor Sipho Nkabinde, White Sisinyi, Addington Dlova, John Mothibi Gaanakgomo, John Fakazi Mdakane, Sisa Njikelana, Prema Naidoo, Alan Fine, Sam Kekene, Suresh Nanaby, Cederic Mayson, Rob Adams, John Nkadimeng, Jacob Wesi, Joe Slovo, Hymie Barsel, Rusty Bernstein, Nelson Mandela, Albert Luthuli, Mahatma Gandhi, James Thompson Bain, Cornelis Broeksma, David Garnius Wernick, Burger Vermaak, Colin Wade, James Thompson Bain, General Christiaan de Wet, ZK Mathews, Walter Sisulu, Oliver Tambo, Helen Joseph, Moses Kotane, Robert Sobukwe, Cecil Williams, Reverend Douglas Thompson, Joe Thloloe, Rusty Bernstein